How Come Every Time
I Get Stabbed in the Back
My Fingerprints
Are on the Knife?

JERRY B. HARVEY

How Come Every Time I Get Stabbed in the Back My Fingerprints Are on the Knife? And Other Meditations on Management

Jossey-Bass
San Francisco

Jossey-Bass books and products are available through most bookstores. To contact Jossey-Bass directly, call (888) 378-2537, fax to (800) 605-2665, or visit our website at www.josseybass.com.

Substantial discounts on bulk quantities of Jossey-Bass books are available to corporations, professional associations, and other organizations. For details and discount information, contact the special sales department at Jossey-Bass.

Manufactured in the United States of America on Lyons Falls Turin Book. This paper is acid-free and 100 percent totally chlorine-free.

Credits appear on page 261.

Library of Congress Cataloging-in-Publication Data

Harvey, Jerry B.
 How come every time I get stabbed in the back, my fingerprints are on the knife? and other meditations on management
/ by Jerry B. Harvey.—1st ed.
  p. cm.—(The Jossey-Bass business & management series)
 Includes bibliographical references.
 ISBN 0-7879-4787-3 (alk. paper)
 1. Organizational behavior. 2. Communication in organizations.
3. Leadership. 4. Organizational learning. I. Title. II. Series.
 HD58.7 .H377 1998
 658.4'092—dc21

                98-58117

FIRST EDITION
HB Printing 10 9 8 7 6 5 4 3 2 1

The Jossey-Bass
Business & Management Series

CONTENTS

ACKNOWLEDGMENTS

Martin Heidegger once said that most of us flawed human beings have to confine ourselves to developing a single idea during our lifetimes (Barrett, 1979). I can't speak for others, but I have found that Heidegger's dictum certainly applies to me. In a previous book called *The Abilene Paradox* (Harvey, 1988c), in my current efforts, and in virtually everything else I have written over the past twenty-five years, I have explored the idea that truthful communication enhances our spirits and that lies and miscommunication either bruise or destroy our souls, regardless of the organizational setting. Simultaneously, I have explored the manner in which our inborn need for acceptance and our reciprocal fear of ostracism and rejection contribute to our proclivity to lie or to tell the truth.

What Heidegger didn't say is that none of us develop our Idea alone, in a vacuum, without assistance from others. God knows, a lot of people—some wittingly and others unwittingly—have helped me develop various aspects of the

Idea that "the Good Lord—out of confusion, compassion, appreciation, administrative errors in the Idea Assignment Division, or other reasons beyond the limits of my comprehension—saw fit to offer me" (Harvey, 1988a, p. 37).

For starters, I have had the good fortune to have some extraordinary mentors. Robert R. Blake was one. He was one of the most exciting, interesting, provocative, creative, and challenging professors I ever met in my many (and I do mean many) years as a university student.

Behind his back, and out of affection, awe, and more than a little envy, his graduate assistants, of whom I was one, awarded him the moniker Rapid Robert. I am not absolutely certain why we assigned him that appellation, but I think it may have come about because of an 11:00 A.M. class he had every Monday, Wednesday, and Friday morning at a location approximately a quarter mile from his office at the University of Texas at Austin.

Regularly, at approximately 10:45 A.M., he said to his minions, "Let's all go have a cup of coffee before class." Then he and his ragtag entourage of acolytes trooped across the campus, with him in the lead and the rest of us following like bonded geese. We collided with Guadalupe Street, one of the busiest thoroughfares in Austin. Apparently paying not one whit of attention to signal lights or onrushing vehicles, Rapid Robert would forge his way across, dodging traffic, as we, in fear for our lives, desperately tried to maintain the pace. Once safely across, we headed for a well-known campus watering hole that had swinging doors. As we burst through the doors, a server, who was accustomed to the thrice-weekly avian parade, saw us coming and placed steaming cups of coffee on the lunch counter, which was located near the far end of the dining room. We sat for a couple of minutes, taking cautious sips from our respective cauldrons.

Suddenly, in response to an invisible internal clock, Rapid Robert would announce, "We have to get moving." With roiling cups in hand, we rushed through the kitchen in the rear of the restaurant, handed the cups to a sweating dishwasher, and disappeared out the back door, which was located adjacent to the garbage cans. By semi-sprinting the last few yards, we always made it to class on time, rarely with more than milliseconds to spare.

One morning, after a particularly harrowing episode, one of us got up the nerve to ask him, "Dr. Blake, why are we doing this?" His reply was, "Everyone has to take a break sometime."

It was a real break for me to have had the opportunity to work with him and to experience his genius regarding the mysteries of human behavior in general and traffic patterns in particular.

Another of my mentors was Leland P. Bradford. A protégé of Kurt Lewin, Lee was director of National Training Laboratories, better known as NTL. As you may know, NTL was one of the major organizations that spearheaded the development of the basic theory and practice of laboratory education, T-groups, sensitivity training, organizational development, and, in fact, the field of applied behavioral science in general. As far as I am concerned, Lee was to the applied behavioral sciences what General Grove was to the Manhattan project.

For reasons only he would know, Lee hired me as a twenty-six-year-old neophyte directly out of graduate school. He then gave me virtually free rein to consort with the "gods" of my field, including such seminal contributors as Douglas McGregor, Dick Beckhard, Warren Bennis, Ken Benne, Bob Tannenbaum, Jack Gibb, Warren Schmidt, Chris Argyris, Gordon Lippitt, Ronald Lippitt, Bill Dyer, and Carl Rogers. Lee also was a fanatical golfer who introduced me to the intricacies of the game. Damn, did I ever learn a lot working for and with him. Unfortunately, I didn't succeed in learning nearly as much about golf.

To my dismay, my relationships with both of those esteemed mentors soured. At first, I blamed the demise totally on them and their manifold shortcomings. As you might surmise from reading the chapter "How Come Every Time I Get Stabbed in the Back, My Fingerprints Are on the Knife?" I no longer ascribe to my initial verdict. I wonder, though, why I was surprised that my fingerprints could be identified by a well-trained investigator. After all, I placed them there. Furthermore, I now realize that they were barely smudged.

My third mentor was Ira Iscoe, who supervised my doctoral dissertation. Like Carl Jung, who fell into a state of depression after splitting with his mentor, Freud, I went into a purple funk after a rocky divorce from Rapid Robert. Totally dispirited, wallowing in the throes of self-pity, and fully convinced of my intellectual ineptitude, I was on the verge of dropping out of graduate school and giving up my quest for that elusive Holy Grail called a doctoral degree.

At that point, Ira offered to assume the role of directing my doctoral dissertation. To this day, I don't know why. I doubt that Ira has ever read what I wrote. His assistance consisted primarily of phoning me every couple of days and asking how my research was going. Generally I would reply, "It's hopeless." With equal consistency, he would retort, "Goddammit, Harvey, I'm sick and tired of hearing you moan and groan. Get off your butt and get moving." Ira always had a way with words.

Today, Ira is the godfather of my son and one of my very best friends. I love him dearly.

In addition to having been graced with exceptional mentors, I have more than my fair share of extraordinary colleagues who contribute to my work on the Idea, which I hope I have nourished as faithfully as it has nourished me.

Erik Winslow, the longtime chair of the management science department of The George Washington University, is the best academic administrator I have ever known. I say that because he is the only person I have ever met in that role who understands the difference between administering a collegium and managing a bureaucracy. He has had the good sense not to attempt to manage us but has done everything he could do to help me and my equally bizarre colleagues do our work. Erik is misplaced, though, because he should be a dean or a university president. I suspect that he isn't, nor ever will be, in one of those roles because he would set standards of excellence for academic leadership that are beyond the reach of most who hold those positions.

Peter Vaill, who is exceedingly bright and exceptionally well educated, has provided me with continuous encouragement, inventive substantive input, warm friendship, and the full resources of his steel-trap mind.

Elliott Jaques, a good friend who I believe is doing the best and most creative work ever done in the field of organizational behavior, has been a constant source of good-humored inspiration and profound intellectual challenge. After I spend a couple of hours engaged in brain-rattling conversation with Elliott, I frequently lapse into a state of such consuming reverie that my automobile, like a well-trained horse, takes me to its familiar stable at Reagan National Airport rather than to my home ten miles away in McLean, Virginia.

Other friends and colleagues, listed in no particular order of importance, whom I particularly want to acknowledge for their contributions are John Lobuts, Tony Petrella, Sue Eichhorn, Warner Burke, Linda Webb, Vlad Dupre, Joe Cotruzzola, Michael Catlett, Herb Koplowitz, and Sidney Edwards.

In addition, I have been blessed throughout my academic career with unusually competent graduate assistants. Colleen Jones, Eleni Stavrou, Stephanie Lamberti, and Ruth Axelrod are four who have made primary contributions to my attempts to understand the nuances of organizational behavior described in the ensuing chapters. Robert Aitken helped out immeasurably by checking the final details and proofing the manuscript.

Finally, I could not have completed any of my work without the loving support of my family: my son, Scott; my daughter, Suzanne; and my wife, Beth.

Acknowledgments

Scott is a lawyer—a very competent lawyer, as a matter of fact. Despite that blot on our family's quest for decency and overall respectability, he is immensely creative and an exceptional writer. He has graciously shared both of those qualities with me in my work. But, most important, he is very funny and has a way of making me laugh whenever I am ready to chuck it all and report to the Great Administrator in the Sky that my one Idea has disappeared to places unknown.

Suzanne has served as an editor in residence for me. She has an extraordinary, almost scary, insight into the human condition, and both thinks and writes with passionate precision. Although she has been ill during much of the preparation of the manuscript, she, as much as anyone else, has helped me come to grips with the absolute essence of the Idea that I have been attempting to nurture.

Finally, I am most grateful for the loving support of my wife, Beth. She, too, is a lawyer who thinks and writes with disciplined precision. She also leads our family (which includes another lawyer, my daughter-in-law, Stephanie) in stimulating dinner-table discussions of torts; and, believe me, there is nothing like a rousing discussion of torts to get one's digestive juices flowing. In many ways, she is both my toughest critic and my staunchest defender. We have been married thirty-five years, and, if I have anything to do with it, we will be married for thirty-five more. She is the love of my life. This book is dedicated solely to her.

Amen.

THE AUTHOR

Jerry B. Harvey is professor of management science at The George Washington University in Washington, D.C. He is a graduate of the University of Texas at Austin, where he earned an undergraduate degree in business administration and a Ph.D. in social psychology.

Prior to joining the faculty of The George Washington University, Harvey spent nine years on the staff of the NTL Institute of Applied Behavioral Science in Washington, D.C., as program director for its management programs and as deputy director of the institute.

A diplomate of the American Board of Professional Psychology and a founding member of the Organizational Development Network, Harvey has served as a consultant and keynote speaker for a wide variety of industrial, governmental, religious, educational, and voluntary organizations. He has published many articles in the fields of organizational behavior and education. He is the author of the well-known book *The Abilene Paradox and Other Meditations on Management* (New Lexington Press, 1988) and is featured in three widely used organizational videos (all from CRM Films) based on his work: *The Abilene Paradox* (1984), *Group Tyranny and the Gunsmoke Phenomenon* (1989), and *The Asoh Defense: Managing Blame and Forgiveness* (1989).

Currently, Harvey is engaged in the exploration of ethical, moral, and spiritual issues of organization.

INTRODUCTION: IT'S NOT MY DOG

A number of years ago, our family—which consisted of me, my wife, and two preschoolers—rented a condominium adjacent to a pristine, crescent-shaped, sandy beach near Ocean City, Maryland. Because our lease commenced several weeks after the official tourist season had concluded, few outsiders were to be found. In comparison to the hurly-burly one finds during the middle of the summer, the resort area was deserted.

A Walk, a Man, and a Dog

At approximately 6:30 A.M. on the first morning of our foray into the world of surf and sand, I awoke before the remainder of the troops had sprung into action and decided to take a solitary stroll along the beach in preparation for the chaos that inevitably attends having two small children gamboling amidst an onslaught of waves and sharks. I don't know whether you have visited that particular area of Maryland's Eastern Shore during the off-season. If you have, you know that at daybreak, when you step onto the beach from an oceanside condominium and look toward the ocean, about all you are likely to see is the rising sun, a few clouds, several fishing vessels, and an uncluttered horizon. There is a tranquil ambiance born of quietness, vastness, and solitude. It was in that peaceful context that I began my journey.

As I meandered along the beach, I suddenly became aware of two unidentifiable, animate objects several hundred yards ahead. I continued toward them until I was approximately twenty feet away and then stopped. Before me was a short, bald-headed man, whose weight I would conservatively estimate at 320 pounds. He was wearing a green checkered bathing suit that looked as if it had been fashioned from an old tablecloth a frugal owner might have discarded from a neighborhood pub. He sported a magnificent handlebar mustache. And he was engaged in the unlikely task of digging an enormous hole in the sand with a small purple plastic bucket. Adjacent to him was an equally obese male Labrador retriever, which was engaged in digging a proportionally large hole with his massive front paws.

Observing that kind of activity is not how I usually start my mornings, so I stood transfixed and quietly watched. The man clearly was an Olympic-caliber digger, because he had created a hole large enough that someone with the proper inclination could deposit a thirty-gallon garbage can

2

into it with room to spare. The dog was equally competent, at least as far as dogs go. Indeed, he had burrowed so deeply into the sand that only his flanks and tail were visible when he was engaged fully in his endeavor, the purpose of which was not even remotely apparent to me.

The dog and man worked in tandem. One would dig while the other rested, and vice versa. They never dug at the same time. Periodically, either the man or the dog would emerge from the cavern he was constructing and rest. Simultaneously, the other, as if activated by an unseen timing mechanism, would commence to mine great volumes of sand. In many ways, they reminded me of the ditch-digging machines one observes at construction sites.

As I observed this unusual phenomenon, I began to have the uneasy feeling that I was an uncompensated extra in an Andy Warhol movie or, more likely, the subject of a *Candid Camera* episode. However, after I had watched the man and the dog for ten minutes without being accosted by Allen Funt (the host of the *Candid Camera* television show), curiosity overcame me. So I approached the man and said, rather tentatively, "I beg your pardon, Sir. As you may have noticed, I've been observing for quite a while and I'm very curious. Are you and your dog digging for anything in particular?"

He looked up and replied, rather curtly I thought, "It's not my dog."

I waited, perhaps a full minute, for some sort of elucidation; but none came. Instead, the man and the dog resumed their tandem efforts.

3

As they alternately appeared and disappeared into their respective burrows, I said with a sense of increasing desperation, "Oh, so it's not your dog?"

"Right," he replied. "It's not my dog." And he continued to dig.

After five more minutes of silence, I realized that our conversation was over. I had said my piece, he had said his, and the dog could only bark.

I felt that I was an unwitting party to some sort of existential absurdity, the exact nature of which eluded me. So, feeling the primal anxiety that existential crises generate, I literally ran home, burst noisily into our beach-level apartment, woke my wife, and in an excited, somewhat agitated voice said, "Beth, I have participated in an absurdity. You've got to hear about it." She sat up in bed, half-asleep, and Scott and Suzanne ran into the room shouting, "What's wrong with Daddy this time?"

Ignoring both her lethargy and their queries, I proceeded to recount the whole affair, describing the bald-headed obese man, the handlebar mustache, the green checkered bathing suit, the purple plastic bucket, the huge Labrador retriever, and the mysterious pattern of tandem digging. Eventually I reached the punch line: "His answer was, 'It's not my dog.' Don't you think that's absurd?"

Beth's reply was trenchant and to the point. "Absolutely," she replied. "I think it's completely absurd that you would expect the poor man to know what motivates somebody else's dog."

For the second time that morning, someone had splashed the metaphorical equivalent of cold water in my face. As a result, I spent the remainder of my vacation uneasily contemplating the two answers.

To my surprise, the more I meditated about them, the more I realized that the replies of both the mustachioed digger and my beloved spouse were much more stimulating than my question, because each forced me to explore a new and fundamentally different set of assumptions about the nature of the situation in which I found myself. Nevertheless, it took more than a little psychic energy to reach—and to accept—that conclusion.

Throughout my life I had been taught, and have accepted without question, that asking the "right" question is a fundamental requirement for developing creative, new, unexpected, fecund solutions to problems new or old. After my encounter on the beach, however, I realized for the first time that asking the "wrong" question can stimulate equally productive venues for exploration. It is the generic process of questioning itself, not whether the questions are "right" or "wrong," that stimulates learning. For that reason, the process of questioning many of the basic assumptions that I have employed in an effort to understand the nature of organizational life is central to the content of this book. Asking myself and others, "Are you and your dog digging for anything in particular?" and then examining the unexpected reply, "It's not my dog," is more than a trivial intellectual exercise. I believe it is integral to learning anything of importance, organizational dynamics included.

5

Meditations at the Beach

Therefore, in Chapter One I begin the process by asking myself the penetrating question, How come every time I get stabbed in the back, my fingerprints are on the knife? That cutting-edge query arose from discovering that no matter how often I have felt betrayed by others in an organizational setting, the truth is that I have always played an *active* role in my own downfall. In fact, I have reached the conclusion that neither I, nor anyone else I know, nor any organization to which I have belonged, has ever truly been stabbed in the back. We have been frontstabbed, sidestabbed, or even murdered. Believe me, though, each of those experiences is fundamentally different from being stabbed in the back. Furthermore, I am convinced that it is important to know the nature of the difference if we and the organizations we create are to function effectively.

Building on the train of thought established in Chapter One, I began to muse in Chapter Two about the biblical Judas, whose name is synonymous with betrayal, an act that is generally accepted as a form of backstabbing. If I am correct in my conclusion that backstabbing doesn't occur, Judas didn't stab Christ in the back; nor was he a traitor. All of those present, Jesus included, colluded in setting Judas up to do the dirty work that the organization needed to have done. Initially, I found that my conclusions regarding the role of Judas and his organizational colleagues, the "spin doctors," were very disturbing. First, they required me to reevaluate cherished religious beliefs I long

6

have taken for granted. Second, casting religious (but not spiritual) concerns aside, I didn't like the implications of the Last Supper's dynamics for our lives in contemporary organizations. If the historical Judas wasn't a traitor, then neither are the present-day Judases whom we scapegoat in our organizations. Rather, they are symptomatic of our efforts to divert attention from *our* complicity in contributing to major organizational problems. See what *you* think. I would be interested in learning about your reactions.

While writing Chapter Two, I realized that the "spin doctors"—the disciples—just sat on their duffs and did nothing when confronted with an organizational crisis of epic proportions. Consequently, in Chapter Three, I look at the dynamics of sitting on our duffs and compare them with the dynamics of standing for something in our day-to-day organizational lives. It is a very short chapter, but for me it stands on its own.

In Chapter Four, I explore the ways in which I believe that educators in general, and management educators in particular, can engage in the process described by the chapter's title, namely, not*teaching. Ultimately, the chapter deals with my conviction that teaching, as we usually practice it, gets in the way of learning and that "good teaching" is an oxymoron. Assuming that you take the content seriously, as I do, the skills for managing competently can't be taught but can be learned. All in all, the chapter adumbrates the lessons I have learned from years of not teaching management and organizational behavior, both as a university professor and as a consultant to organizations.

In Chapter Five, "Prayers of Communication and Organizational Learning," I explore the role that prayer frequently plays in organizational behavior. I doubt that I define prayer as you do, but I'm *uncomfortable* enough with my definition to consider the issue of organizational prayer as worthy of exploration. From my thirty years of experience as a consultant to organizations, I know that many major decisions in ostensibly secular organizations are actually made on the basis of prayers to the deity. I also know that a large number of ultimately destructive organizational decisions are made because organization members avoid prayerful consideration of issues that confront them. Based on my observations of the subtle communication that occurred between the Labrador retriever and his mustachioed colleague on the beach, I often wonder whether dogs also pray. I suspect that they very well might.

Chapter Six, "This Is a Football: Leadership and the Anaclitic Depression Blues," deals with the way in which our inborn need to be emotionally connected with others and our reciprocal need not to be abandoned or ostracized by others are integral to the exercise of effective organizational leadership. From my point of view, the chapter may be one of the more important pieces that I have written, because the role of anaclitic depression is central to virtually everything I have produced, starting with *The Abilene Paradox* (1988c) and working up to the present. Lord knows, I have experienced the kind of anaclitic depression that is characteristic of individuals who are dying, not living, in organizations that are incompetently led.

In Chapter Seven, "What If I Really Believe This Stuff?" I explore the relationship of the anaclitic depression blues to a variety of commonplace organizational processes. For instance, I discuss why so-called normal, bell-shaped distributions of human performance actually reflect abnormal, anaclitically depressed behavior on the part of organizational members. I also discuss why *real* distributions of performance in high-performing organizations are always bimodal rather than symmetrical and why it is necessary for high-performing organizations to maintain a cadre of low performers in order to facilitate overall organizational excellence. Finally, I explore why objectivity on the part of a leader creates an anaclitically depressed workforce that ensures organizational mediocrity.

In Chapter Eight, I build on the work of the preceding two chapters and engage in musing about "the elephant in the parlor." In this chapter, I discuss the seminal work of Elliott Jaques, a metaphorical elephant whose presence most of us who are engaged in the theory and practice of organizational behavior desperately try to deny. I am convinced that his work is the most creative, intellectually demanding, and organizationally significant of any in the field of organizational dynamics. Yet relatively few managers, academicians, consultants, students, or bartenders know of, or are aware of, what he has produced. For approximately thirty-five years, the elephant has been trumpeting, "It's not my dog" and "How can you expect anyone to know the motivation of someone else's dog?" Despite the elephant's roars, most of us have avoided the questions he has asked and, even more, the replies he has generated. I hope to do my part in rectifying what I believe to be our near-phobic fear of both dogs and elephants.

"Social Intervention as the Process of Releasing Flatus in the Confines of Religious Institutions," Chapter Nine, was written in collaboration with Dr. Bobby Lee Bemus, a long-time Texas colleague who doesn't exist. More accurately, he doesn't exist physically, although Carl Jung might contend that he lives and works in my shadow (Campbell, 1971). Leaving the details of his exact status aside, I wrote the chapter with ol' Bobby Lee because I sure as hell am not going to be the primary author of the kinds of ethereal arguments he makes. Many people who have had access to drafts of our work don't like it. Ronald Markillie, for instance, one of my closest friends and an esteemed colleague, said simply, "It stinks." Other friends, colleagues, and a few enemies have sent us copious suggestions for additions to it, some of which have been so obscene that *I* was offended by them. Although Bobby Lee and I have incorporated several of their ideas into the manuscript, I think you might be interested in knowing that none of them wanted us to give them *any* formal recognition for their contributions. Bobby Lee and I share the ambivalence of both our critics and our collaborators. Consequently, we hope you like it but would not be at all surprised if you don't.

Given the brevity of Chapter Ten, "Ode to Waco," you might reach the conclusion that I consider it to be trivial. I hope not, because I don't. I wrote it while listening to the spokespersons for two warring religious institutions, the FBI and the Branch Davidians, comment on their respective strategies for coping with the situation in which they found themselves. The more I listened, the more I realized that the two organizations shared value systems that were virtually identical. Yet, despite the enormous similarities of their core beliefs, they were prepared to annihilate one another. As you probably know, one eventually did destroy the other, in part, I think, because the two principals had so much in common. As good old Willie Shakespeare barked many years ago, "Lord, what fools these mortals be!" (*A Midsummer Night's Dream* 3.2). Since "these mortals" are ultimately "we," I wonder if Willie, in his wisdom, could have helped the principals avoid the debacle in Waco had he taken on the project as a consultant.

I conclude the book with Chapter Eleven, "When We Buy a Pig," which explores the tragedy that frequently occurs when organizations hire and worship no-nonsense managers. I take this chapter very much to heart. Maybe you will, too.

The book has an Afterword, "In Memory of Suzanne." I wrote it during a period of great personal sadness and overwhelming despair. I debated with myself as to whether it should be included, but I have no ambivalence now. Sometimes parts of books, even books dealing with organizational behavior, are written as much for the author as for anyone else. This chapter is for me and—God bless her—for Suzanne.

Other Elements of the Landscape

While revolving around life in organizations, the material in this book tends to be very moralistic in places. Being a confessed preacher at heart, I don't apologize for that. I want you to know, though, that I am aware of it and am acutely sensitive to the potential dangers it poses to my efforts to communicate with you. My fondest hope is that whatever moralism I exhibit is a gentle reflection of my lifelong concern with organizational issues that are ethical, moral, and spiritual in nature and is not a misguided expression of narrow-mindedness that is characteristic of a religious zealot. To state this differently, I hope that my moralistic themes are not oppressive or relevant only to individuals from a single religious or spiritual tradition or relevant only to those who have a religious or spiritual tradition.

I can't avoid, nor do I want to deny, the fact that my religious background combined with my penchant for spiritual inquiry has had an enduring impact on the way in which I view all aspects of organizational life. I hope that, at best, you will experience the moralism, with all of its limitations and its universality (if any), as a spiritual expression of the type that Joseph Campbell described when he explored *The Masks of God* (Campbell, 1970). And, if my hope is not fulfilled, I ask both your forbearance and, ultimately, your forgiveness.

How Come Every Time I Get Stabbed in the Back My Fingerprints Are on the Knife?

In a related vein, similar to my previous book (*The Abilene Paradox,* 1988c), this is primarily a compilation of meditations, some of which are disguised as essays. When I speak of meditations, I mean that I have tried to share some concerns, ideas, and issues related to organizational behavior that I believe may be worthy of mulling over and thinking about. Alternatively, I have not tried to provide ironclad or even tentative solutions for much of anything. I think that my hesitancy to do so stems from two sources. First, the more experience I have gained from the study of organizational behavior, the less sure I have become about what I know. Second, Jack Gibb (1964) has pointed out in his work on trust theory that giving advice to others, as opposed to sharing ideas and information with them, is an expression of distrust. Therefore, when I see authors offer advice-laden versions of "Ten Sure-Fire Techniques for Achieving Organizational Success and Solving All Your Problems Without Risk, Stress, or Strain," I know that they have little trust and respect for the readers and even less for themselves. Although I may sympathize with authors who do that, I don't care to join them.

As some of you may know, I am a storyteller at heart, so much of this book is built around stories. Although my official job title is Professor of Management Science, I do not consider myself to be much of a scientist. I am convinced, though, that a good story is a scientifically valid way to explore many facets of human existence, including life in organizations—assuming, of course, that generic science ultimately is concerned with the search for reality and truth. Therefore, I focus much more on stories than on the results of double-blind experiments. Although I have enormous respect for those who work within the framework of rigorous scientific method, I personally have not found that life is a repeated measures design. Furthermore, I have found at times that a disproportionate number of double-blind experiments dealing with what I consider to be the important concerns of organizational life are just that: doubly blind.

As I have grown older (and have, I hope, grown in ways other than age and waist size), I have discovered to my delight that stories have several qualities of which I have only recently become aware.

To begin with, stories give me a lot of information about myself and my role in society. In many ways, I feel as if I am the sum and substance of my stories. I wonder if you feel that stories do the same for you?

In addition, stories tell me something about the nature of the world in which I live, even though I frequently don't know what the story is trying to tell me when I first hear or participate in it. Apparently, I am not the only one who has encountered that dilemma. In his wonderful novel *The Living End,* Stanley Elkin (1979) describes a discussion that some of heaven's inhabitants have with God. In effect they ask, Why did you create a world with so many puzzling, incomprehensible, and paradoxical features? "Because it makes a better story," God replies (p. 144).

Like the characters in Elkin's novel, my memory and file cabinets are loaded with stories relating to events in which I have been a participant but of which I have yet to understand the point. Nevertheless, as both the stories

14

How Come Every Time I Get Stabbed in the Back My Fingerprints Are on the Knife?

and I marinate in the ebb and flow of life, I'm sure the point will come to me or, if not to me, to someone who, I hope, will elucidate its meaning to me and others.

As I have said before (1988c), I attribute much of my interest in storytelling to my maternal grandfather, with whom I had the good fortune to spend a lot of time. When as a child I visited him and my grandmother during summer vacations, the whole family gathered on the porch during Sunday afternoons. With him presiding from his rocking chair and all participants armed with flyswatters, we would, in his poetic words, "Swat flies and swap lies."

I want to be sure that the meaning he, and we, attached to the latter part of that Sunday afternoon activity is not misunderstood. Wilfred Bion, a great psychoanalytic storyteller, described lies as "formulations known by the initiator to be false but maintained as a barrier against statements that lead to a psychological or emotional upheaval" (1970, p. 97). That's certainly not what my grandfather and we had in mind. To us, a lie was, and is, not a violation of the truth. Rather, a lie is a slight expansion or elaboration of the truth for a couple of reasons: first, to provide a creative emphasis and elucidation of the truth and, second, to make more bearable the terrors that the truth often holds. That may be descriptive of some aspects of my stories, too, but I don't think you will have any difficulty in ascertaining when those slight expansions or creative elaborations occur.

Ultimately, I have attempted to produce a set of meditations about organizational issues that are worthy of contemplation, rather than a list of prescriptions for personal or organizational success. My expectations for the book are therefore very limited. At best, I would be honored if on occasion you might be moved to say to yourself or to someone you know, "I'll be damned. I never thought of that before."

With that in mind, I invite you to locate your flyswatter and join me on the front porch. If you don't want to come alone, you are welcome to bring a dog—even if it doesn't belong to you.

CHAPTER ONE

Some Thoughts About Organizational Backstabbing or How Come Every Time I Get Stabbed in the Back My Fingerprints Are on the Knife?

Backstabbing—defined as "an attempt to discredit by underhanded means, such as innuendo, accusation or the like"—seems to be prevalent in all kinds of organizations, including families, churches, businesses, governmental agencies, academic institutions, and voluntary associations. People in managerial leadership roles, in particular, seem both to be interested in it and to complain about it a lot.

For instance, an acquaintance who holds a top management position in a well-known corporation and who is noted for his proclivity for traversing even the most spacious hallways of his company's headquarters with his back ensconced firmly against the wall, asked me the other day if I knew anything about the phenomenon. I told him that I didn't fancy myself as an expert, although I certainly possessed enough experience to be one.

You see, I have been stabbed in the back more than once—to be exact, 131 times more than once, not counting near misses and superficial flesh wounds. If, perchance, you should be skeptical enough of my estimate that you feel the need to hire a CPA to audit it, you might find that the figure I quoted is slightly exaggerated; but it sure seems that high to me. Whatever you decide, my good friend Wilfred Bion has reminded me that you need to take part in a significant event only once to learn from it, assuming that you approach the problem of learning with the proper attitude and discipline (Bion, 1969).

The Case of the Red Bird Reading Group

Although I probably don't remember the first occasion when the blade was deposited in the thoracic region of my spine, I do recall the circumstances under which I became fully aware of the pain and suffering that participation in the event entails. I was six years old at the time and had recently entered the first grade as a conscript in Mrs. Elizabeth Sanders's Red Bird reading group. I thought that Jimmy Bob Reed was the culprit. For sure, I know he spread the ugly rumor that I had not done my fair share of the work on the clay turkey that Jimmy Bob and I were assigned to construct for the Thanksgiving exhibit. I am equally certain, however, that I was the one who trekked barefooted through the chicken lots of my grandparents' farm to collect the colorful plumes Mrs. Sanders said "provided a touch of absolute authenticity" to our artistic endeavors. I also know that Jimmy Bob spread the rumor, because several Red Birds informed me straight out that he told them he was planning on doing it "just to take me down a notch or two." In addition, a couple of other Red Birds chirped coded messages, the meaning of which, in retrospect, was about as difficult to interpret as the sound of the siren perched atop the local fire station. Although they differed widely in their styles of chirping, each of the messengers provided the warning in "the strictest of confidence" because none of them wanted to get Jimmy Bob's feathers ruffled. Furthermore, each also said that he was doing it because of his undying love and affection for me.

Despite the primitive sense of foreboding that their information generated within me, I always acceded to their requests for confidentiality. There is a certain thrill inherent in being privy to a secret. In addition, I gained a modicum of security from knowing that so many of the flock thought well of me and that I had faithful friends who were intent on looking after my welfare.

Consequently, although I knew Jimmy Bob was up to something that wasn't going to win any Nobel prizes for decency, I never said anything to Jimmy Bob, either directly or indirectly, about what I knew or suspected. To the contrary, every time I saw Jimmy Bob, I gave him my most self-confident smile and said, "Hello, Jimmy Bob, old pal. We put together a great turkey, didn't we?" In return, he flashed his gap-tooth, duplicitous grin, for which he was justly famous, and responded, "We sure did, Jerry, old buddy," after which I went on my way, trying to keep in mind that I had learned in Sunday School how Sweet Jesus had particular affection for little kids like me who turned the other shoulder blade.

To put it mildly, Jimmy Bob was clever. In fact, I didn't even know I'd been stabbed until we Red Birds received our introduction to the perils of performance appraisal in the form of our report cards. It was only when Jimmy Bob received an "outstanding" in Cooperation and I got a dreaded "needs improvement" along with a written explanation addressed to my beloved mother ("Jerry must learn to be more responsible for doing his fair share when he works with others") that I knew for certain that a knife had been lodged squarely in my trapezius.

At that moment, I decided to take matters into my own hands and set the record straight. I went directly to Mrs. Sanders, told her the whole appalling story of how Jimmy Bob had stabbed me in the back, and awaited the act of justice I was sure would be forthcoming. I approached her with great confidence, because I knew from observing the statue of Justice atop the courthouse that Justice, though blind, carries a sword in her hand.

It was with absolute shock that I found that Justice may be deaf or may wear earplugs, but she certainly isn't blind. In fact, Justice apparently looks at events through a microscope. More to the point, Mrs. Sanders didn't take my word for how the knife achieved its peculiar location. Instead, to my utter surprise, she proceeded to take a box labeled "Learner's Fingerprinting Kit" from the top drawer of her desk and, as she put it, set about to "investigate the case."

Within the hour, she fingerprinted all of us Red Birds, dusted the knife for telltale markings, and then, to my

22

How Come Every Time I Get Stabbed in the Back My Fingerprints Are on the Knife?

ultimate despair, announced that she had identified the culprit—namely, me. She went on to say that although the knife contained smudges of prints that might possibly belong to other Red Birds—Jimmy Bob included—the evidence was far from definitive and would never stand up to either public or judicial scrutiny. She said that in fact my fingerprints, and only my fingerprints, were clearly identifiable on the knife and opined that I must have attempted to stab myself to death in some sort of self-destructive frenzy.

Adding to my melancholy, most of my Red Bird colleagues, some of whom had served as messengers and others of whom had witnessed the proceedings from a distance, lent credence to her bizarre explanation by nodding their beaks in apparent agreement. I say "apparent" because several of the most prominent beak rockers subsequently flew by my feather-filled desk to let me know that they knew exactly what Jimmy Bob had done and, furthermore, that they really didn't agree with Mrs. Sanders's assessment. According to them, they only appeared to agree because they didn't want to get either Jimmy Bob or Mrs. Sanders on their cases. In addition, they knew that I, being the good bird I was—and unlike the dastardly Jimmy Bob or the insensitive Mrs. Sanders—would understand the reasons for their benign deception and would not hold such a minor transgression against them.

Despite the weight of evidence against me and notwithstanding my tender age, I had the presence of mind to ask Mrs. Sanders how she had reached the unusual conclusion that I had stabbed myself in the back when I couldn't reach

23

far enough over my shoulder to remove the offending object—which by now was causing me considerable misery—virtually none of which was physical.

Staring over the rims of the half-glasses she used for reading, Mrs. Sanders sighed ever so slightly and replied, "You will have to figure that out by yourself, young man. The criminal mind is beyond my comprehension."

Since it also was beyond my comprehension, I can't say with any sense of conviction that the intervening 130 stabbings occurred any differently. It didn't seem to matter whether I thought the perpetrator was Jimmy Bob Reed, who maimed my academic reputation; or Dannie Dell Deemer, who torpedoed my budding romance with Flo Ann Hamilton, the comely cheerleader for the Dangerfield Wampuscats; or Corporal Earl T. MacBee, who engineered a delay in my promotion to squad leader in the 249th Potato Loading Platoon; or Dr. Samuel Floyd Windom, who masterminded my dismissal from the ranks of Confederated Consultants, Inc. Each time, my fingerprints and only my fingerprints were clearly identifiable on the offending weapon. The event became so commonplace that I was convinced I must be the only person in the world who could stab himself where he couldn't scratch.

As I look back on my experiences, the pattern for getting stabbed in the back was completely predictable. It was so predictable, in fact, that it brought forth uncomfortable memories of B. F. Skinner's insightful dictum (1938) that the major difference between rats and people is that rats learn from experience. Consequently, in a state of abject depression, I set about to identify and describe that pattern

24

How Come Every Time I Get Stabbed in the Back My Fingerprints Are on the Knife?

in the margins of my bloody pocket calendar. In addition to engaging in solipsistic inquiry, I also interviewed a number of friends, associates, and a few enemies in an effort to ensure that my experiences with what one of them euphemistically termed "the bureaucratic spinal tap" weren't unique. What follows is a summary of my musings, the title of which stems from where the musings were recorded in my calendar and not from my perception of their importance; because deep down, regardless of what you and others may conclude, I believe they deal with archetypal essences.

Marginal Musings
on Backstabbing

Although dictionaries define backstabbing; although the etymology of the word is clear; and although political scientists, group theorists, organizational researchers, and psychiatrists have discussed the impact of collusion, deceit, and duplicity in a wide variety of organizational settings; I know of no literature that deals with the underlying dynamics of backstabbing *per se*. (For discussions of collusion, deceit, and duplicity, see, for example, Safire, 1986; Machiavelli, [1532] 1950; Bion, 1961; Argyris and Schon, 1978; and Peck, 1983.) Such a dearth is surprising when you consider the intense emotions that the phenomenon generates in a multiplicity of cultures (Safire, 1986). Having spent the greater part of my adult life as a consultant to organizations, I have come to realize that an understanding of those issues that cannot be discussed in polite company (or polite companies) is as important as an understanding of those issues that can be discussed, and sometimes more important. Therefore, I wonder what it is about backstabbing that makes it undiscussable?

Thinking about that question, I realize that I have met a lot of people from organizations who claim they have been stabbed in the back, and even more who claim to have witnessed such attacks. However, I have yet to meet anyone who admits to having stabbed someone. Because even the most callous of criminals—murderers included—frequently confess, sometimes with pride, to committing other kinds of crimes, I believe that the absence of organizational backstabbers who are willing to own up to their transgressions provides a significant clue to the qualities that make backstabbing so undiscussable. Specifically, it may be that the accepted, traditional definitions of backstabbing stem solely from the biased viewpoint of the alleged victims, messengers, or witnesses, all of whom might have something to hide, and not from the perceptions of the person alleged to be the stabber—who may have nothing to hide and may, in fact, be altogether innocent of the crime of which he or she stands accused.

Consequently, I am going to describe backstabbing, not as a discrete event that can be summarized in a single sentence, but as an ongoing process that involves multiple parties. I am also going to attempt to describe it in a way that I think Mrs. Sanders would appreciate, because the more I ruminate about backstabbing, the more I am con-

26

How Come Every Time I Get Stabbed in the Back My Fingerprints Are on the Knife?

vinced that Mrs. Sanders learned a lot more from employing her Learner's Fingerprinting Kit than she ever revealed during her conversations with me.

For better or worse, and as unsparing in its description as Mrs. Sanders was in the conclusions she reached about me, here is the process as I now understand it. Incidentally, as I discuss backstabbing I capitalize a number of terms because they refer to generic roles participants play—roles that in a sense are independent of the individuals who play them.

The Process of Backstabbing

Backstabbing usually commences not when the actual stabbing occurs but when the Potential Victim hears a rumor or gets a direct message from a third party, generally a trusted friend or associate, about the planned assault. Occasionally, though, it begins with nothing more than a gnawing feeling of foreboding in the pit of the Potential Victim's stomach. This is the type of gut-level intuitive signal you receive when you have a pretty good idea that something is amiss, of what that something may be, and of who is probably involved in it, but for whatever reason you are afraid to act on the information that your gastric processes are supplying you.

I say "Potential Victim" because it is important to understand that Potential Victims can't become Real Victims of backstabbing until they actually get stabbed. That seems obvious to me now, but for some reason it eluded me when I nested with various flocks of Red Birds over the years. To put it in the colorful language of my colleague, Erik Winslow, "If you can see it coming toward you, you can't get stabbed in the back."

When the warning comes directly, the Messengers generally preface it by avowing their support for the Potential Victim and their disrespect for the Potential Perpetrator (who, like the Potential Victim, can't be a Real Perpetrator until he or she actually perpetrates). Messengers also tend to begin or conclude their missives with an admonition that "this information must be held in the strictest of confidence." Sometimes they buttress their restrictive covenants with elaborate and sensible-sounding explanations as to why confidentiality is necessary to protect both the Potential Victim and themselves. Such demands for confidentiality frequently are supported by some version of the threat, "If you use my name or even indicate to anyone else that you know about this, I'll deny I ever said it, and, furthermore, I won't try to protect you from the Potential Perpetrator—or any other Potential Perpetrator—in the future." Evidently, the organizational world is full of Jimmy Bobs who are perceived to be extremely dangerous if they get their feathers ruffled.

Concerned about losing the support of his Messengers if he violates the oath of confidentiality he has taken with them, the Potential Victim does not confront the Messengers with their collusion in his potential stabbing. For instance, the Potential Victim does not let the Messengers know how their demands for confidentiality limit his freedom to use their information in the best way possible to prevent himself from getting stabbed. Nor does the Potential Victim inform the Messengers about how their failure to tell the Potential Perpetrator that they believe his actions are unkind, immoral, unfair, destructive, or downright mean sends an implicit signal to the Potential Perpetrator that he can act with impunity. Consequently, the Messengers, if not confronted by the Potential Victim about their collusion with the Potential Perpetrator, generally opt to say nothing, and thereby encourage the Potential Perpetrator to carry out the attack. In addition, the colluding Messengers do so under the guise of trying to help the Potential Victim. In the words of my dear Mama, "With friends like that, who needs enemies?"

Once the Potential Victim tacitly agrees to protect the Messengers from having to choose whether or not to confront the Potential Perpetrator, and if the Messengers opt not to confront the Potential Perpetrator, the Messengers cease to be the Potential Victim's friends and acquaintances and become accomplices in the crime. Less euphemistically, they become Sidestabbers. I doubt that many Messengers really want to become Sidestabbers. Yet, with the Potential Victim's tacit blessing and encouragement, they do so anyway.

Similarly, being fearful of the Potential Perpetrator and apparently unaware that the Potential Perpetrator is just that—a Potential Perpetrator—until he carries out his nefarious act, the Potential Victim does not confront the Potential Perpetrator with his knowledge of the Potential

Perpetrator's plan to attack. By failing to do so, the Potential Victim encourages the Potential Perpetrator to express his potential for destructiveness and evil. In similar fashion, through his silence, the Potential Victim colludes with the Messengers in encouraging the Potential Perpetrator *not* to develop his potential for behaving with decency and rectitude.

Because of his failure to confront either the Potential Perpetrator or his sidestabbing cohorts, the Potential Victim places his fingerprints on the knife and smudges theirs. Consequently, he ceases to be an innocent party to the stabbing and, like the Sidestabbers, whose original intentions may have been honorable, paradoxically becomes an accomplice to his own assault! As Mrs. Sanders said, "The criminal mind is difficult to comprehend."

By becoming an accomplice, the Potential Victim thereby destroys much of the evidence connecting the Potential Perpetrator and the Sidestabbers to the crime. He destroys it both in his own mind and in the minds of others—including Witnesses, who have observed the developing debacle from a distance while falsely contending that they have not in any way been involved. For that reason, the Potential Victim's and only the Potential Victim's fingerprints are clearly imprinted on the knife, a fact that becomes important when it comes to assigning blame in the organization's "court of law."

Then, his back solicitously turned in self-imposed blindness so as to provide a safe and easy target, the Potential Victim gets stabbed and is transformed into a Real Victim. Blood flowing, he continues his journey into Real Victim status by retreating to the security of the organization's infirmary, which usually is located in the Human Resource Department, for an extended period of recovery. During his recuperation, he is visited by various Sidestabbers and an occasional Witness. Most of them, in turn, attempt to salve both the Real Victim's wounds and their own consciences with sympathetic commiseration and reassurance that they share his belief that the apparent perpetrator is truly a scoundrel of the first magnitude and that he—the Real Victim—is a paragon of innocence, whose purity approaches and maybe surpasses that of Mother Teresa.

Despite the convoluted expressions of concern from sympathetic visitors, and despite the treatment offered by HR specialists (most of whom echo the principals' birdcalls that backstabbing is an individual phenomenon, thereby establishing themselves as Professional Sidestabbers), the Real Victim feels the overwhelming sense of depression characteristic of someone who has been stabbed in the back. As best I can ascertain, he feels such depression because he *has* been stabbed in the back.

Furthermore, being blind to his complicity in the crime, the Real Victim repeats the cycle again and again until he has no more blood to give. Eventually, he becomes the casualty of a bloodless coup and spends the remainder of his organizational days slithering down hallways, back against the wall, eyes rotating like radar antennae—a sallow, lifeless shadow of his former self and essentially a noncontributor to the organization's mission.

Other organization members, observing the deterioration of the Real Victim and suffering self-encouraged stab wounds of their own, join the ranks of Real Victims on the periphery of the organization's hallways. Eventually, virtually all members of the organization become, for all practical purposes, predominantly occupied with the task of protecting their backs rather than working to achieve the avowed goals of the organization. Over long periods of time, many Real Victims become so frightened and confused that they cease to defend their upper backs and become obsessed with defending parts of their anatomy located posterior to their anterior pelvises. When that occurs, coping with the injury caused by failure to use a well-known defense having the euphemistic acronym *CYA* becomes one of the *only* shared goals around which members of the organization organize their efforts.

Backstabbing as a Social Disease

Looking at the pattern I have described, it is clear that *backstabbing is not a crime committed by a solitary individual acting in isolation*. Rather, it is an intricate kaleidoscope of collusive deception that involves the complicity of a wide variety of Perpetrators, Messengers, Witnesses, and Victims. One might even say it is a peculiar form of social disease whose outcome, like the outcome of most social diseases, is thoroughly antisocial.

Understanding the collusive nature of backstabbing, I now believe I know one important reason why the phenomenon has received so little systematic study. Real Victims, in particular, prefer to blame the ostensible Perpetrators for the crime and thereby avoid the pain that comes from confronting the reality of their own complicity and the complicity of their erstwhile friends and associates in spreading the disease. In effect, we Real Victims have provided ourselves with a subtle conceptual alibi by defining backstabbing as something that another person does to us. Thus we don't have to run the risk of having to cope with the ethical, moral, and spiritual issues that emerge from being aware of the part we play in the mutilation of our own spines. More important, perhaps, we don't have to explore the implications of playing a role that subtly encourages us and others to abdicate our potential for doing what is just and good, not only to others but also to ourselves.

I think that both Messengers and Witnesses also appreciate and give their full-fledged support to our traditional dictionary definition of backstabbing. As long as they can blame the traditional stabber, commiserate with the traditional victim, and thereby keep secret their traditional complicity in the crime of spreading the disease, they don't have to suffer the primitive fear that comes from owning up to their involvement in the process; nor must they face the genuine risk that comes from deciding not to participate in the backstabbing process, regardless of the circumstances.

It is no wonder that my fellow Red Birds didn't want the perceptive Mrs. Sanders on their cases.

The Underlying Causes
of Backstabbing

What then is the basis of the anxiety, the abiding fear that leads us to avoid confronting ourselves and others who are potentially involved in backstabbing? Well, strange as the explanation may seem, I believe it stems from our existential fear of being separated from others—of being ostracized, of being truly alone—and our reciprocal desire to be connected with and emotionally supported by others.

For instance, numerous authors have pointed out that we all need emotional support from others to survive, both physically and mentally, and we all know how much it hurts to be ostracized, isolated, and lonely. (For further discussion of this issue, see Chapter Six.) Because of our knowledge—knowledge based on the hard experiences of everyday living—we will do nearly anything to avoid running the risk of rejection. We even seek to avoid the real risk of being rejected by those Potential Perpetrators and Sidestabbers who we suspect, or know, may ultimately be out to hurt us.

I now believe Mrs. Sanders was both correct and incorrect when she said that the criminal mind is difficult to comprehend, at least when backstabbing is involved. At one level it is not. Participation in our own backstabbing is the result of our desire to be accepted and our reciprocal fear of being rejected by Potential Perpetrators and Messengers if we confront them with what we believe or know to be true. Since our desire for acceptance is universal, our fear of being rejected, also universal, is easily understand-able. What is not comprehensible to me is our fear of being rejected by those who we believe will ostracize and reject us regardless of the truth with which we confront them (and ourselves) and regardless of the kindness, de-cency, skill, and compassion with which we do it. So I ask myself, and you, Who wants to be associated with people like that? If you come up with a satisfactory answer to my question, please call me—collect.

Differentiating Backstabbing from Stabbing, Sidestabbing, and Frontstabbing

While you ponder that question, you also might like to consider the implications of the fact that stabbing oneself in the back is not the same as committing suicide. You can kill yourself in lonely isolation without the cooperation of others. However, you need the collusion of at least two additional parties—the Potential Perpetrator and at least one Messenger—to maintain the fiction that you have been stabbed in the back and to convince the rest of the world that the primary blame lies with someone other than yourself. Stated differently, it may take two to tango, but it takes three to set up the conditions for stabbing one-self in the back.

Such triadic collusion is required because if only two people are involved, an action that in other circumstances might be called backstabbing, sidestabbing, or frontstabbing becomes stabbing, period.

Stabbing, to be more precise, is an attack against another party undertaken by a solitary Stabber without the complicity or foreknowledge of others, including Messengers, Potential Victims, or Witnesses. Given its solitary, unprovoked, random quality, at least from the point of view of the Real Victim, stabbing has about the same relationship to being an authentic human encounter as does getting killed in an accidental fall in one's bathtub. Although Stabbers rarely take action in formal organizations, when they do we generally describe their behavior as an act of "terrorism" or "murder."

In contrast to the direct attack of stabbing, sidestabbing involves the process of suppressing confrontation between Potential Victims and Messengers, and between Potential Victims and Potential Perpetrators. Thus, sidestabbing occurs when a Messenger demands that a potential Victim keep the Messenger's identity and the contents of his message secret from the Potential Perpetrator—and the Potential Victim complies. The Messenger, aided and abetted by the acquiescence of the Potential Victim, not only fails to protest to the Potential Perpetrator about the imminent backstabbing but also effectively blocks the Potential Victim's avenues for doing so. The Messenger thus drives a knife into the Real Victim's side, and does so with the Potential Victim's full cooperation.

Alternatively, if more than two parties are involved and if the Potential Perpetrator takes his planned action despite being confronted by the Potential Victim or Messenger, his behavior is called frontstabbing, and the Potential Perpetrator becomes a Frontstabber. That act involves an attempt by one or more individuals to dominate others who have made it clear that they don't want to be subjected to such exercises (abuses) of power.

William Barrett (1979, p. 219) has termed those acts of domination "the expression of one's will to power" and has described the destructive impact on the souls of those who engage in it. In the civilized, day-to-day language of contemporary organizations, however, the expression of our will to power more frequently is called "healthy head-to-head competition" or "a contest of wills." In a less civilized form, it is known as "war." Maybe that's why, in so many contemporary organizations, there are individuals who are known for their cutting remarks, others who are identified as the organization's spear carriers, and still others who have honed reputations as axe men.

Do you want an example of organizational frontstabbing? Not long ago I spoke with a friend who had worked for an organization whose employees (including those in managerial roles) voted, by a margin of 80 percent to 20 percent, to take an across-the-board 20 percent pay cut to reduce personnel costs so that the organization could compete more successfully in the marketplace. By their action, the employees hoped to ensure that neither they nor their colleagues would lose their jobs and that they would meet the shareholders' needs for a sufficient return on their investments. However, the CEO, in collaboration with a small group of top and middle managers who opted to support him, refused their offer and fired 20 percent of the workforce. According to the CEO, "It was very important that management's prerogative to manage as it saw fit not be compromised by sentimental human considerations." Given the context in which the firings occurred, the CEO's action was a prototypical expression of the will to power. It was organizational frontstabbing at its best, carried out by a force of well-trained spear carriers and axe men.

Backpatting as an Alternative to Backstabbing

If a Potential Victim develops what we generally call courage and, as a consequence, opts to confront either the Potential Perpetrator or the Messengers, he may find that those whose rejection he so feared will respond with backpatting, which is an unequivocal expression of support and friendship. Backpatting occurs because, not surprisingly, the Potential Perpetrator and Messengers frequently need the emotional support of one another and the Potential Victim as much as the Potential Victim needs theirs. In fact, in the absence of such support, all parties frequently suffer from anaclitic depression, a form of depression caused by being emotionally isolated from others, and one that frequently leads to serious physical illness or death. Consequently, each has a vested interest in receiving support from the others (see Chapter Six for an extended discussion of anaclitic depression).

Despite our inborn need to receive emotional support from others, the transformation from the roles of Potential Perpetrator, Potential Victim, or Potential Sidestabber to the role of Backpatter is not always easy. It may evolve during a process of difficult, soul-searching confrontation that takes place over an extended period of time. Alternatively, it may occur nearly instantaneously when the potentially conflicting parties confront one another in various combinations and find, generally to their total surprise, that none of those involved in the potential stabbing really want to take part in it. If you are interested in pursuing the latter puzzling phenomenon in greater depth, I discuss it in *The Abilene Paradox* (Harvey, 1988c), which describes how and why organization members who agree that they want to be friends with one another frequently engage in senseless disputes that violate the desires of all those involved.

Regardless of whether it is achieved slowly or instantaneously, backpatting is ultimately an expression of altruism. According to George Vaillant (1974), altruism, the act of doing to others what one would like to have done to oneself, is an adaptation to life that is necessary not only for the well-being of individuals but also for the survival of civilized society.

Interestingly enough, I know of few organizations that have formal or informal ethical prohibitions against backstabbing, sidestabbing, or frontstabbing. To the contrary, many organizations implicitly condone the practices. For instance, many organizations have norms that say it would be unethical for Potential Victims to confront the Potential Perpetrators because they might accuse the Potential Perpetrators unjustly. Similarly, many organizations have norms that say it would be unethical for Sidestabbers and Witnesses to get involved in fights in which they are not directly involved. And Frontstabbers frequently receive both formal and informal organizational acclaim for being powerful, hard-nosed, no-nonsense managers and leaders.

Alternatively, I do know of formal ethical prohibitions against offering the kinds of support that backpatting ultimately generates. For instance, in most academic organizations, cheating is defined as giving altruistic assistance and backpatting support to others on examinations. Honor, on the other hand, is defined as withholding help from those who need it to survive (Harvey, 1988c).

Avoiding the Knife in the Back

Before becoming aware of the integral role they play in their own downfall, Potential Victims frequently ask, "What can I do to prevent others from stabbing me in the back?" Once aware of their complicity in the process, Potential Victims often ask the peculiar-sounding but ultimately practical question, "What can I do to keep from stabbing myself in the back?" At a deeper level they may be asking,

"What can I do to increase the possibility of getting patted on the back rather than having a knife deposited in it?" Or, perhaps, at the deepest spiritual level, they are asking, "What can I do to enhance the possibility of experiencing the pleasure that comes from patting others on the back rather than cutting them up in an organizational knife fight?"

Whatever the questions that are ultimately being asked, I am aware that I have no guarantees when it comes to answering them. However, given the collusive, antisocial nature of backstabbing, I do know that breaking the pattern of destructive complicity by taking some sort of action that allows (but can never ensure) at least the possibility of backpatting is an absolute necessity. Although I can't truthfully say I have had a lot of experience taking such actions, I do know, on the basis of my experiences and experiences reported to me by others, of several approaches that have been successful:

1. Confronting Potential Perpetrators with your awareness of their intentions. If my understanding of the backstabbing process is correct, Potential Perpetrators, if confronted, will either (a) retreat in a manner reminiscent of the proverbial neighborhood bully faced for the first time by a fearless Potential Victim, (b) become Frontstabbers, or (c) be transformed into Backpatters. Whatever happens, they can't stab a Potential Victim in the back.

2. Confronting Messengers about their role in the potential crime. Such confrontation, I think, requires several actions:

◇ Refusing to abide by the Messengers' requests to keep the content of their messages secret.

◇ Explaining the reason for your refusal. For example, you might say something like, "If you give me the information under a restriction that makes it difficult or impossible for me to solve the problem, there is no reason to give it to me in the first place. However, if you want to give it to me and then let me use my own judgment as to how to employ it, I will accept it with thanks."

◇ Pointing out the way in which the combination of the Messengers' failure to express their avowed disagreement with the Potential Perpetrator's actions and their attempt to prevent you from freely using the information contained in their messages makes them parties to the potential crime. Also let them know that such actions on their part simultaneously ensure that they cannot contribute to the development of potential altruistic, backpatting relationships among all parties involved.

Regardless of what the Messengers do in response to that kind of confrontation, they can't stab you in the side.

3. Confronting yourself about your role in the process. Basically, such confrontation requires that you must be willing to run the paradoxical risk of being rejected or ostracized by others in order to keep from stabbing yourself in the back. At the same time, it demands that you be willing to participate in the soul-soothing experience of

42

How Come Every Time I Get Stabbed in the Back My Fingerprints Are on the Knife?

backpatting, with all the risks that are inherent in being vulnerable to others.

Of course, Potential Victims can always opt to do nothing and get stabbed in the back.

Backstabbing, Risk, and Faith

You probably can think of many other alternatives that I and the people I interviewed haven't heard about or considered. I do know, though, that whatever alternative you choose will be fraught with risk and ultimately will be an expression of faith—which I define as an approach to living that we opt to follow without guarantees about the outcomes of our choices. Such acts of faith, by definition, are individual, unique, unteachable, and, ultimately, spiritual in nature. I am convinced that you and I and everyone else have to make our own choices about how we express our faith in action when it comes to dealing with our potential for organizational backstabbing and backpatting.

Whatever choices we make, though, have risks associated with them and, therefore, cannot be reduced to an exercise of skills or techniques (Barrett, 1979).

Being aware of all that, I know that neither I nor anyone else can tell you how to express your faith in the corridors of your own organization. I can tell you one thing for certain, however: if we invest our energy in pursuing the convoluted faith that leads us to become Real Victims, we will have to live much of our organizational lives the way my acquaintance who inspired this chapter spends his—with our backs against the wall, trailing streaks of crimson behind us, and with the full knowledge that, regardless of who conducts the investigation, our fingerprints will always be on the knife.

44

How Come Every Time I Get Stabbed in the Back My Fingerprints Are on the Knife?

CHAPTER TWO

The Spin Doctors: An Invitation to Meditate on the Organizational Dynamics of the Last Supper and Why Judas Was Not the Traitor

Note: Appreciation is expressed to Eleni Stavrou-Kostea for her assistance in developing this chapter.

As I thought more about the process of backstabbing, I asked myself, Who has an undeserved reputation for being a well-known, world-class backstabber? After racking my brain awhile, I came up with the biblical Judas.

Judas. When you hear that name, regardless of the organizational context in which it is uttered, what words do you associate with it?

I suspect that most of us for whom the name is familiar, irrespective of our religious affiliations or secular organizational memberships, will select some variation of "traitor." In fact, wherever you go throughout much of the world, the name Judas is synonymous with betrayal, disloyalty, untrustworthiness, and backstabbing.

If you are not convinced of that, look at life in those ubiquitous organizations we call families. How frequently do you hear prospective dewy-eyed parents announce to friends and relatives, "If it's a boy, we're going to name him Judas"? I know that I have never known any parents who attached the appellation "Judas" to their progeny, nor have I been acquainted with anyone who seriously considered doing it. Furthermore, those who out of ignorance or for other reasons might consider breaking the taboo are solicitously warned in books such as *20,001 Names for Baby* that to name one's baby Judas is "Very unusual, probably because of the traitorous apostle Judas Iscariot" (Wallace, 1992, p. 313).

Likewise, if you were informed that your work organization's representative in important, life-and-death negotiations with a competitor had the nickname "Judas," I doubt that you would be filled with unbounded joy or that your level of confidence in his—or her—suitability for the role would soar to untrammeled heights.

The name Judas doesn't seem to stimulate our desires to participate in public displays of affection, either. A kiss may be just a kiss in a lot of settings. However, if you are in the Mafia, or any other organization for that matter, a Judas Kiss is something that few of us want to receive, regardless of the organization to which we belong and irrespective of our role within it. Otherwise known as the Kiss of Death, such a bussing portends the premature, violent demise of the recipient; so even the most passionate members of organizations try to avoid the experience. When Judas is involved, the line differentiating a kiss of life from a kiss of death cannot be ascertained by studying osculatory physiology.

Finally, distaste for the name Judas is not limited to humans. It is my understanding that even sheep try to avoid sticking their necks out when following any goat named

48

How Come Every Time I Get Stabbed in the Back My Fingerprints Are on the Knife?

Judas, although the frequency with which lamb chops appear on restaurant menus serves as a visible reminder of how often they fail in their resolve. Given that failure, I doubt that they derive much satisfaction from knowing that Judas goats, which lead lambs to slaughter, inevitably are slain. Using academic argot, neither Judas goats nor their faithful followers achieve tenure-track positions.

Yes, Judas has a lousy reputation. But I have concluded that, negative though it may be, his reputation is largely undeserved. In fact, I am convinced that Judas is a prototypical scapegoat whose reputation as a traitor was the result of a concerted public relations campaign. Furthermore, I believe that the campaign was conducted by an early group of spin doctors who wanted to put their unique spin on the story and angle it to suit their particular predilections and interests.

Some may feel that my calling the disciples "spin doctors" is both behaviorally inaccurate and inappropriately contentious. I believe, however, that the term may be poignantly descriptive. William Safire (1986, p. 8), for example, reports that it "was coined on the analogy of *play doctor,* one who fixes up a limping second act [of a play], and gains from the larcenous connotation of the verb *doctor,* to fix a product the way a crooked bookkeeper 'cooks' books." Given its etymology, I think *spin doctors* is a particularly apt term to describe the behavior of the disciples, who clearly wanted to divert attention from their collusion in the premature demise of their leader and the suicide of their longtime colleague, Judas.

I imagine that the disciples also wanted to avoid confronting the implications of their leader's possible complicity in contributing not only to his own death but also to the abusive use and consequent death of Judas. At least they may have done so if they experienced anything similar to the fear and trembling that I—a lifelong, semi-tub-thumping Southern Baptist—experienced while thinking the thoughts (and abandoning the disthoughts, rethoughts, and unthoughts) required to produce this chapter.

From reading the minutes of the meeting called the Last Supper, I suspect that the disciples' actions were grounded in a couple of additional, rather mundane motives. One was a desire to cover their duffs, "duff" meaning not only one's buttocks or rump but also "to give a deliberately deceptive appearance to; misrepresent; fake." Less euphemistically, they were trying to protect their proverbial backsides by covering up a lie. (See Chapter Three for more on the subject of covering one's duff.)

I believe that another motive was to create a well-honed organization that would help them advance the belief system set forth by a supposedly unblemished leader (Wilson, 1992). Apparently the disciples didn't comprehend (or care about) the enormously destructive impact that scapegoating their colleague Judas and then labeling him as a traitor would have on the behavior of future organizational members. Paradoxically, the efforts of the disciples to protect their own backsides and their organization's image have served as a powerful, yet morally questionable, model of ethical behavior that members of many future organizations, both secular and religious, have unthinkingly emulated.

50

The more I think about it, the more I am convinced that the behavior of participants in the organizational meeting we now call the Last Supper was virtually identical to the behavior of those of us who participate in meetings of contemporary families, churches, businesses, and voluntary associations. That is, like the participants in the Last Supper, we possess the sophisticated moral potential required to act with responsible caring and concern for *all* members of our respective organizations. At the same time, we frequently lack the courage to express the potential we possess. Thus, we end up needlessly sacrificing one another on an altar of contrived organizational necessity when other, more constructive alternatives are clearly available.

Regardless of whether we choose to risk exercising our potential for moral organizational action in the present, I am convinced that we must exercise it in the future. Only then can we make our organizations both function more effectively and develop spiritually. In fact, unless we develop our potential for collective moral behavior and incorporate it into our day-to-day organizational life, I am convinced that we will live and work in ineffective, morally stagnant institutional complexes of interlocking organizations. Such dysfunctional organizations constitute what Scott Peck describes as a world full of undiscovered, more positive possibilities that are waiting to be born (Peck, 1993).

I'm aware that I have made a number of rather sweeping assertions. I invite you to meditate on their validity and implications as you read the following account of the Last Supper. In my opinion, it is one of the most important organizational meetings in recorded history. As part of your meditation, I hope you will think about the discussion that I believe might have ensued among the disciples in their effort to justify their subsequent actions both to themselves and others.

Approaching the Story of the Last Supper

The minutes of the Last Supper, taken from *The Living Bible: Paraphrased* (1971), follow. Although you can find biblical summaries of the event in Matthew 26:20–29, Mark 14:17–25, Luke 22:14–38, and John 13:18–30, I have constructed a composite, using the version in John as the basic framework. I have noted when I deviated from John, and have made a concerted effort not only to include the major interpersonal and group dynamics of the story but also to sequence them in a way that makes chronological sense. When I have had to make changes in verb tense or add words to make the story flow, I have surrounded those changes with brackets.

As you read, you may want to place a replica of Leonardo da Vinci's famous painting *The Last Supper* in front of you. However, doing so may be somewhat disconcerting if your reaction to the painting is similar to mine. Preferring circular, square, or rectangular seating arrangements for dinners, I, for one, have more than a little difficulty accepting da Vinci's compliance with the demands of artistic expression by having everyone at the table sitting in a straight line. In addition, knowing that the

Last Supper was the Passover Seder yet leavened bread is on the table, that the ostensibly impoverished disciples are wearing colors that result from the use of very expensive dyes, and that the room is decorated in Renaissance style (R. Axelrod, personal communication, July 12, 1998), makes me wonder whether Leonardo might have consistently wet his whistle on schnapps as he struggled to resolve the nuances of artistic interpretation.

Putting that possibility aside, whatever geometric arrangement you select to seat the participants, remember that John, the organization's recording secretary, sits adjacent to Jesus, with Peter on the other side of John. (If you use da Vinci's depiction, John is to the right of Jesus, and Judas is at Peter's right, as you face the painting.)

If you want the written account of the meeting really to come alive, role-play it with thirteen people, following the description in the printed account as closely as possible. For example, have the person who plays Jesus dip a piece of bread into a sauce and actually give it to the person who plays Judas. Also have each disciple ask Jesus aloud, "Am I the one?" and have Jesus answer as the account in the Bible implies. If possible, have some fun doing it. I have found that exploring the unknown is a lot more illuminating when carried out in the light spirit that enlightenment seems to require.

Finally, as you read, please try to forget the theological or historical baggage that you may be carrying around from previous experiences with the story. If you are not religiously inclined, or if you come from a religious tradition for which the Bible is not significant, you may want to read

53

or role-play the story as the Last Dinner Meeting of the Executive Committee. Within that framework, you may also want to dress everyone, metaphorically or actually, in their daily work clothes.

Whatever approach you take to the task, keep in mind that a traitor is "one who betrays a trust; . . . hence, one who acts deceitfully and falsely." Pay particular attention to which participants *actually* act deceitfully and falsely and, again, try to ignore preconceived notions you may have about who the "guilty" parties are. I have found that form of ignore-ance *(sic)* difficult to carry out.

Apparently I am not the only one who has experienced that kind of difficulty in ignoring the preconceptions that I bring to the table. For example, Hugh Schonfield, the author of *The Passover Plot,* a somewhat rabble-rousing interpretation of the events leading to Jesus' crucifixion, seems to have difficulty accepting the possibility that the disciples were aware of the moral dilemma facing them. For instance, he says that when Judas made his exit to betray Jesus, "the company in general thought nothing of this" (1965, p. 133). Likewise, in *The Sacred Executioner,* Hyam Maccoby says of the moment when Jesus passed the sop to Judas as a means of identifying the traitor, "We can not suppose that *all* the disciples heard Jesus explaining his sign, or they would not have been ignorant of the betrayer's identity" (Maccoby, 1982, p. 125).

Anyway, difficult as it may be, I hope you will try to disregard your past interpretations of the event's organizational dynamics and see if you reach any new insights or interpretations about what happened or may have happened.

54

The Last Supper
(Composite Version)

"I am not saying these things to all of you; I know so well each one of you I chose. The Scripture declares, 'One who eats supper with me will betray me,' and this will soon come true" (John 13:18). "I must die. It is part of God's plan. But, oh, the horror awaiting that man who betrays me" (Luke 22:22). ["]I tell you this now so that when it happens, you will believe on me["] (John 13:19).

Now Jesus was in great anguish of spirit and exclaimed, "Yes, it is true—one of you will betray me" (John 13:21). Sorrow chilled their hearts and each one asked, "Am I the one?" . . . Judas, too, . . . asked him, "Rabbi, am I the one?" And Jesus . . . told him, "Yes" (Matthew 26:22 and 25).

Since I was sitting next to Jesus at the table, being his closest friend, Simon Peter motioned to me to ask him [again] who it was who would do this terrible deed.

So I turned and asked him, "Lord who is it?"

He told me, "It is the one I honor by giving the bread dipped in the sauce." And when he had dipped it, he gave it to Judas, son of Simon Iscariot.

As soon as Judas had eaten it, Satan entered into him. Then Jesus told him, "Hurry—do it now."

None of the others at the table knew what Jesus meant. Some thought that since Judas was their treasurer, Jesus was telling him to go and pay for the food or to give some money to the poor.

Judas left at once, going out into the night (John 13:23–30). [*The Living Bible: Paraphrased,* 1971, pp. 773, 795, 831, and 853]

Given that the twelve remaining participants sat on their duffs while Judas went out the door and into the night, ostensibly to betray Jesus, what must have occurred among the disciples *after* Jesus' death for the story to have been written? Stated differently, how did the disciples manage to construct an alibi that most of us apparently accept as valid?

Here is my best guess, and it involves a group of early spin doctors in action.

The Spin Doctors at Work

"Did you hear?" asked Thomas. "Judas did hang himself. It's official. What we heard was no rumor."

"Well, what did you expect?" responded James, with more than a slight edge to his voice. "We encouraged the damned guy to leave dinner knowing full well that he was up to no good."

"Encouraged? How did you reach that conclusion?" mumbled Bartholomew.

"Oh, come on, Bart," continued James. "Jesus said that one of us was going to betray him and that he was going to die. He even said that whoever did it was in for some real misery. One by one, each of us asked if he was the guilty party, and Jesus said, 'No.' Then Judas asked, 'Is it I?' and Jesus said, 'Yes, Judas, it's you.' After that, Jesus said to him, 'Now get up and go about your business and do it quickly.' To the best of my knowledge, none of us is deaf, blind, or stupid. When Judas left the room all of us had a pretty good idea about where he was going and what he intended to do. Not one of us did anything except stare at the ceiling or ask for the matzah. We just sat on our respective duffs and let him go out the door. It's no wonder that he committed suicide. He must have been in total despair once he realized that we had colluded with Jesus in using him that way. Lord, he must have felt abandoned. You can argue all you want that we sacrificed him to achieve the long-term goals of the organization, but as far as I'm concerned what we asked of him went far beyond what any God-loving organization can decently demand."

Hot tempered as usual, Peter shouted, "Don't put me in the 'duff' group. I had no idea what Judas was going to do."

"And don't give me that crap," retorted John. "You practically leaned over in my lap just before Jesus told Judas to leave and asked me to repeat what Jesus had said. As you have so conveniently forgotten, I repeated Jesus' statement to you and the others word for word. You heard what I said, everyone else in the room heard what I said, and, as much as I'm ashamed to say so, *I* heard what I said. For those of us who aren't too quick on the uptake, Jesus even said he was going to soak some bread in the sauce and hand it to the culprit, and I don't think I need to tell you who the recipient of that honor was. By just sitting there, playing dumb, acting like we were their loyal friends, we may have deceived Judas and Jesus, but let's not lie to one another. We knew where Judas was headed. If you don't believe me, read the minutes I took during the meeting."

"Well," said Philip, "for the good of the organization, we can't talk ourselves into feeling guilty for some lousy decisions Judas and Jesus made on their own. Judas surprised me, but Jesus didn't. As much as I loved him, Jesus seemed hell-bent on getting himself killed."

Growing more and more agitated, James shouted, "You guys don't get my point. By doing nothing, we *did something*. We *helped* Jesus *use* Judas to carry out Jesus' crucifixion. At the very least, I think we should have had the common decency to tell Judas to get back into the room until we could be sure that he wanted to be used and abused in the way Jesus wanted all of us to use and abuse him. God only knows what might have happened. Judas might have said, 'Thanks guys, I knew something was rotten all along, but I didn't realize that I was about to be betrayed by the organization in the way Jesus had in mind. Jesus, you are going to have to get someone else to help you get yourself killed. I love you too much to do it myself.'"

Taking a deep breath, James continued, "And then Jesus might have said, 'Judas, bless your sweet heart, Old Buddy. You're right. The prophesies could be fulfilled in a lot of ways without your getting killed or labeled as a traitor.' Who knows, we might have saved both of them."

"As long as you want to play 'Who knows?'" interjected Thomas, "Who knows what else might have happened if we had stopped Judas and confronted him? Judas might have said, 'I appreciate your kind concern, fellows, but I know *exactly* what I'm doing. I'm going to appear to betray Jesus so he can get himself crucified. Then I'm going to hang myself so I can take the heat off him and the rest of you. Do me a favor, though, and don't try to stop me. I'm doing it for the good of the organization. I've prayed a lot about what I'm planning to do, and I'm sure that I'm following God's wishes.' Then we would have had two people who claim they sacrificed themselves for us. I don't know about you, but that's one more than I can cope with. No, Judas may have had a decent streak in him, but if he did, I don't want to know anything about it. It's a lot easier for me and everyone else associated with the organization just to hate him straight out. I, for one, don't want to spend the rest of my life worrying that I might have contributed to his or anyone else's evil, and there's no way in hell I want to be a part of setting an organizational precedent that encourages others to think in that way, either."

"Oh, shut up, both of you. I'm sick of hearing all your romantic fantasies about what might have been," screamed Peter. "As much as we may wish otherwise, we didn't stop Judas; and now we have two deaths on our hands. We have to put our petty personal concerns aside and take a long-term strategic view. What can we do to save the organization we have built? We need to put some sort of spin on these tragic events to make sure they work out for the best for all concerned."

Andrew, ever positive, chimed in, "I have an idea. John, you could rewrite the minutes of our meeting in the Upper Room so that whoever reads them would have a difficult time figuring out our complicity in getting Judas and Jesus killed. Changing the minutes certainly would protect the organization's image and reestablish the trust of our field representatives."

"Good idea, Andy. That might work even better if we really bore in on making Judas the fall guy," said Peter. "Drop some hints that he might have had his hand in the till. Claim that we had no idea where he was headed that night. Say, 'The devil made him do it.' But above all, stress the traitor thing. Even though all of us were disloyal and deceitful to both Judas and Jesus, if we focus on Judas's treason and not ours, outsiders might forget our culpability, and with a good PR campaign we might get off scot-free."

"Let me toss another one in the hopper," said Thaddeus. "We could emphasize that the only way the prophesies Jesus was so worried about could be truly fulfilled was by having Judas take the fall. That ought to add speed to the spin."

"But the prophesies could have been fulfilled in a lot of other ways that wouldn't have required that Judas and Jesus get themselves killed," interjected Matthew.

"So what?" continued Thaddeus. "Remember that the trick is to put a positive spin on events until we can get the organization's image back in control."

"Isn't 'trick' a euphemism for an act of prostitution?" asked Matthew. Then, realizing that the glares being directed toward him were not exactly expressions of approbation, he mumbled, "Just an attempt at a little levity, fellows. Sorry, let's move on."

"Matt may be joking," mused Thomas to no one in particular, "but I doubt the whole scheme will work. In addition, whether he's joking or not, I agree with him. I think that what we are doing is perverted . . . evil."

"It's too late to worry about that now," interjected Peter. "Anyway, if you don't like the spin we're putting on things, you can always write your version and try to sell it to the authorities. I doubt they would be willing to pay thirty pieces of silver for it, though."

"Which authorities?" Thomas queried.

"Any authorities," responded Peter. "Any authorities."

An Invitation to Meditate

Black Elk, a Native American shaman, once said, "Whether it happened so or not I do not know; but if you think about it, you can see that it is true" (Neilhardt, 1979 [1932], p. 296).

Accepting the wisdom of Black Elk and assuming that something similar to the events described in my version of the spin doctors' meeting truly occurred, I have been stimulated to meditate about a number of generic issues related to organizational dynamics. Those issues relate not only to our lives in organizations past and present but also to our lives yet to be lived in organizations waiting to be born. Some of these issues are broad in scope; others are quite limited. Some are ridiculous; others are sublime. Whatever their character, here they are.

1. Are many organization members whom we call traitors actually scapegoats? As far as I am concerned, that is a very important question.

On the one hand, traitors, by definition, are disloyally deceptive in their dealings with the members of the organization they betray. Furthermore, we generally assume that the wellspring of traitors' malfeasance is located within them, meaning that traitors have significant character flaws or personality deficiencies that lead them to behave traitorously. Scapegoats, on the other hand, are usually defined as individuals who bear the blame for the malfeasance of others, blame that ultimately resides in those who do the scapegoating. Could it be, then, that organization members frequently brand scapegoats as traitors in an effort to divert attention from the scapegoaters' complicity in the problem for which the ostensible traitors are being blamed? If so, we need another word to describe scapegoats who are falsely identified as traitors.

2. If we do need another word, how about *traigoat,* a combination of *traitor* and *scapegoat?* Thus, a traigoat is someone who is encouraged by organization members to carry out a destructive act on behalf of the organization. Subsequently, that person is blamed by them for doing it and is branded by them as a traitor in an effort to hide the members' complicity in perpetrating the nefarious act for which the ostensible traitor receives sole blame. Such a word also might encourage us to focus our problem-solving efforts on the full range of those involved in the act we call treason.

3. Would the history of the world have been altered significantly had the disciples convinced one another and

Jesus not to abuse Judas in order to achieve the goals of their organization?

4. How would the way in which we make decisions in contemporary organizations differ had the eleven remaining disciples refused to collude with Jesus, Judas, and one another in legitimizing a very destructive model of organizational decision making? More directly, the Last Supper provides a model that encourages us to sacrifice colleagues as a means of disguising our own complicity in contributing to the problem and also teaches us to blame our sacrificial victims for their own demise. Blaming the victim is clearly not a phenomenon that was unrecognized until the advent of modern psychology.

5. Could the Judases of this world ever be accepted as organizational heroes, not traitors, and could a Judas Kiss ever be an act of love? For me, this is not an outrageous question. As I discuss in the chapter titled "What If I Really Believe This Stuff?" incompetents and troublemakers are major contributors to the success of any outstanding organization.

6. Do the Judases of our organizations ever recognize that they have been betrayed by the members of their organization who call them traitors?

7. How many organization members who believe they have been victimized by traitors would understand the probing question I asked in the preceding chapter: How come every time I get stabbed in the back, my fingerprints are on the knife?

8. Is treason a social phenomenon that involves organization members who act in destructive collusion with one another and not the act of unprincipled individuals who work alone?

9. Assuming that treason is a social phenomenon, is the process of attributing it to personality problems or character flaws of the ostensible traitor an even more subtle form of traigoating and another way that organization members try to hide their complicity from both themselves and the world at large?

As I said, these are some of the issues about which I have been meditating. I have reached no firm conclusions about any of them. Perhaps the actions of the spin doctors have aroused other questions or concerns in you. Regardless of the source of your interest (if any), I invite you to join me in the process of meditation.

May you meditate in fear and trembling, in peace, or both. Regardless of how you proceed, I hope you do so with a sense of assurance that the leaders, followers, and peers from organizations of which you are a part will not become spin doctors, use you for their selfish benefit, falsely brand you as a traitor, and then send you out— alone—into the night.

64

How Come Every Time I Get Stabbed in the Back My Fingerprints Are on the Knife?

CHAPTER THREE

On the Ethics of Standing for Something or Sitting on Our Duffs

Note: This chapter was written with Ruth H. Axelrod.

A s I said in the preceding chapter, the disciples sat on their duffs, knowing full well what Judas was up to as he disappeared into the night. None of them took a stand to stop him. If you think about it, what they did is certainly not unusual and not unique to the Last Supper.

In fact, while attending meetings in contemporary organizations, I have become aware that it is very common for one or more exasperated participants to say, "For God's sake, people, let's quit hedging and take a stand on the issue," or "It's time for us to stand up and be counted," or "We ought to stand up to them." In the same or other meetings, I hear members complain, with equal or greater frequency, "We're just sitting on our duffs, doing nothing."

Sitting and standing are such recurring and reciprocal themes of organizational meetings that I began to wonder why. I mean, you never hear participants in meetings say, "Let's quit hedging and take a sit on the issue," nor do historians refer to the battle of Little Big Horn as Custer's Last

Sit. Alternatively, I never have heard anyone say, "We are sitting on our duffs getting a lot of important work done."

Standing and sitting: What do they mean within the context of day-to-day organizational life? Does some sort of reciprocity exist between the two actions that extends beyond the Zen-like conundrum, "Where does your lap go when you stand up?" or "What happens to the wind when it doesn't blow?"

In quest of an answer, I went to my faithful unabridged dictionary. Not to my surprise, I found that, within the context of the previous statements, the word *stand* means to take some kind of a firm, courageous, principled, upright action in the face of an implied threat, conflict, danger, or disagreement.

Then I parsed the meaning of the phrase *sitting on our duffs, doing nothing*. Using the same source, I found that one of the major meanings of the phrase *sit on* is "to suppress or to silence." Finally, I decided to ascertain whether the word *duff* has a relevant meaning with which I was unfamiliar.

According to the same source, *duff* has a variety of connotations. For example, it refers to a lousy golf shot. That particular discovery was no surprise to me. Being an avid golfer whom members of my Saturday morning foursome describe as a *duffer,* I knew that, and my substantial handicap provides objective verification of their description. *Duff* also refers to one's buttocks or rump. Possessing a duff that is more than adequate in size, given my height and weight, I have long been aware of that meaning as well.

One of the definitions was altogether new to me, though. It seems that to *duff* means "to give a deliberately deceptive appearance to; misrepresent; fake." In short, a duff is a form of lie. Thus when we say, "We are just sitting on our duffs, doing nothing," we could as easily be saying, "We are just wasting our energy trying to suppress lies, rather than using our energy to tell the truth, and, therefore, we are accomplishing nothing." This interpretation also implicitly assumes that we have some unspoken truths to reveal, truths that are requirements for accomplishing anything of real value. No wonder we get so exasperated in meetings where we waste energy that could be devoted to getting important work done.

Knowing the precise meaning of the phrase has had a great impact on me. For instance, when I hear myself or someone else say, "We're just sitting on our duffs, doing nothing," I generally ask, "What lies are we sitting on that are getting in the way of the truths that we must discuss in order to accomplish anything of significance?" Once I ask the question, I seldom fail to discover the nature of the lie that is creating the frustrating experience of nothingness about which we are so vehemently complaining.

I invite you to ask the same question whenever you hear the phrase used in any meeting where you are a participant, but I suggest that you make the inquiry only if you are prepared to have your question answered in full. I have found that the great majority of us truth-starved humans prefer to live within the atmosphere of freedom that truth liberates, rather than to waste our energy trying to contain lies that are ultimately uncontainable. For that reason, if you ask the question, you may find yourself in a position similar to that of the individual who asked for a sip of water and ended up getting it from a fire hose. Events like that sometimes happen when you decide to take a stand.

So how are you going to expend your energy during your next meeting when controversial issues are involved? You can opt to take a stand for something and make liberating progress, or you can decide to sit on your duff and do nothing.

Whatever decision you make is one grounded in ethical, moral, and possibly spiritual considerations. And the choice you make is yours alone. I am convinced you can learn that you have a choice to make but that nobody—and that means *nobody*—can teach you *how* to go about making it. That, too, is up to you.

CHAPTER FOUR

Learning to Not*Teach

G iven my firm belief that you can't teach individuals to make decisions and take actions that are central to their lives and the lives of others, one of the most important skills that I have learned as a university professor is how to not*teach. In fact, I gave up trying to teach long ago. Fortunately, I have never given up trying to learn.

This chapter, then, is about teaching, not*teaching, and the process of learning. Please note that here and in subsequent chapters my use of an asterisk between words is not a typographical error; nor does it reflect my incompetence as a speller. It means that the prefix actively negates the stem. Not*teaching, therefore, is a disciplined, active, energetic process of creating an environment that encourages learning.

As you will find, the chapter consists of a series of personal statements, questions, hypotheses, conclusions, descriptions, and observations about learning, teaching, and learning to not*teach. As best I can tell, the series doesn't

73

follow any logical sequence. Not*teaching and learning seldom follow any logical sequence. Teaching does. I hope you find the material to be of interest.

1. The longer I am employed as a professor, the less sure I become as to what a teacher is supposed to do. When students say, either explicitly or implicitly, "Teach me," I become confused, because I seldom feel as if I have anything to teach.

2. Whenever I do think that I have something to teach, I generally am disappointed. Most of the time, others already know it or don't find it useful, interesting, relevant, or profound. And neither do I.

3. I agree with the sentiments Carl Rogers expressed in "Personal Thoughts on Teaching and Learning" (1952). In essence, he contends that nothing of value can be taught but that much of value can be learned. I suppose that's one reason I find teaching so unsatisfying and learning so much fun.

4. I find it ironic that many constituencies of higher education—including students, teachers, administrators, and parents—worry so much about teaching. I suspect that their concern has the purpose of diverting attention from the difficult job of learning, which my colleague Peter Vaill defines as making changes in oneself (1996). Instead, they focus their energy on obsessing about teaching, a process that assumes that the capacity to grow depends primarily on someone else.

5. "Those who can, do. Those who can't, teach." It is a hostile comment, to be sure, but one that for some reason is very popular among those who fancy themselves as doers. Try substituting the word *learn* for the word *teach*. The aphorism now reads, "Those who can, do. Those who can't, learn." When stated this way, the comment loses its hostile quality. In fact, it makes much more sense. I wonder why. Maybe the answer to that question says something about the relative importance of teaching and learning.

6. It also occurs to me that teachers require learners in order to survive, but learners don't require teachers. Maybe that's why teachers emphasize the importance of teaching so much. They are attempting to create a market for their nonessential services.

7. In my discipline, there is a journal called *The Organizational Behavior Teaching Journal.* What if it were called *The Organizational Behavior Learning Journal?* I'll bet that the content of the articles would be very different and a lot more interesting.

8. As a professor, I don't accept responsibility for what others learn. I do take responsibility for what I learn, though. In fact, one of my basic objectives as a professor is to learn. What students learn, if anything, is up to them. I'm always pleased to try to help them learn something if they want to and if I can be of assistance to them in doing it, but I won't accept responsibility for what they learn or whether they learn it.

9. In fact, I am struck by the bizarre willingness on the part of my colleagues to accept responsibility for what their students learn or fail to learn. I know they accept such responsibility, because they frequently ask students, colleagues, and administrators to evaluate their teaching for purposes of promotion and tenure. They get depressed if students don't perform well in their classes. They go into purple funks if their students don't increase their scores on standardized tests. They read books, study journal articles, and attend seminars focused on how to improve their teaching effectiveness. They worry about how to motivate students in the classroom. Each of those acts indicates that, in some way, they believe they are responsible for what their students learn—or fail to learn.

10. Many teachers have the following maxim on a sign atop their desks (or buried in the deep recesses of their brains): "If the student hasn't learned, the teacher hasn't taught." That maxim is quite peculiar, because it clearly implies that the basic responsibility for learning belongs to the teacher. Consequently, if the student performs incompetently, the teacher is at fault. But, following the same logic rigorously, if the student performs competently, the teacher must then get the credit. For all intents and purposes, the student doesn't exist, except as a sort of inanimate, passive receptacle for the teacher's competence or incompetence.

11. In my opinion, any time a teacher accepts responsibility for students' learning, the teacher denies the students' humanity. Stated differently, the teacher doesn't respect the students very much, if at all. Likewise, if students permit the teacher to accept responsibility for their learning, they respect neither themselves nor the teacher. That's why I always make it clear to my students that I'm a professor, not a teacher. I do that because I have found that I don't gain a lot of satisfaction from being either disrespectful or disrespected.

12. When I take seriously the proposition that I am not responsible for what and whether my students learn, I become very anxious, because it forces me to ask, "What is my job?" I wish I could say I've developed a satisfactory answer to that question.

13. I find that grading students is never a satisfying experience. Grading cotton or soybeans makes a lot of sense to me, but grading students does not. Grading deals with teaching, evaluation, accreditation, indoctrination, control, un*thought, dis*thought, and re*thought. It doesn't have much to do with learning. It's demeaning to all parties involved. I get ulcers on the inside of my bottom lip every time I do it.

14. Teachers frequently tell me, "I'm not grading students. I'm grading their work, not them as human beings. There is a difference, you know." If you actually believe that normal human beings can separate themselves from the work they produce, particularly work that is important to them, then I have a suggestion. The next time you receive a performance appraisal and your boss says, "I think that your work was lousy [or great], but please don't take my comments personally," then don't take them personally. Take them impersonally, because your boss's comments apparently don't relate to you as a living, breathing human being. And don't get upset (or pleased) with your boss. Your boss probably was taught to do performance appraisals by a teacher who believed that you could grade students' work without grading students.

15. By the way, Bleuler, a famous psychoanalyst, points out that anyone who splits one's self off from one's self, in the manner that is required to divorce one's self from the quality of one's work, generally is deemed to be schizophrenic (Campbell, 1981).

16. I very much enjoy responding to my students' work. I write them letters, correct their grammar and punctuation, critique the quality of their thinking, curse their ineptitude, applaud their creativity, frown when they do work that is beneath their capacity, and cheer their victories. I learn a lot from responding to them. From everything I hear, so do they. It's just grading them that doesn't make sense. I prefer to stick with grading soybeans and cotton.

17. For their exams, my students are free to express their understanding of the literature and experiences of the course in any way they desire. Historically, they have written poetry, done scientific research, produced essays, sung theories, made movies, danced analyses of variance, presented plays, (literally) juggled constructs, cooked concepts (which the class ate), composed music, brewed

78

How Come Every Time I Get Stabbed in the Back My Fingerprints Are on the Knife?

beer, created works of art, and welded nails. In short, they have learned to work, a process that, according to management theorist Elliott Jaques, is the exercise of discretion and decision making in carrying out a task (1989). Assuming the students are employed or will seek employment in roles that require them to work for a living, I am convinced that their examinations are relevant to carrying out an activity that is required for successful living.

18. Given such freedom, most students have produced extraordinarily competent work. Some have produced work that is very incompetent. Very few have produced anything mediocre. I have thus come to understand that bell-shaped distributions of performance in academia are artifacts of an environment in which teaching is stressed. In learning environments, performance tends to be bi-modally distributed, with most participants, including professors, performing very well, a few performing very badly, and almost none falling into the middle. (For further discussion of performance distribution curves, see Chapter Seven.)

Stated differently, in a learning environment, both students and professors either perform very well or fail miserably. In a teaching environment, the great majority of students and teachers fall into the pedestrian middle. Maybe that's the purpose of teaching—to ensure mediocrity on the part of everyone involved. Dysfunctional bureaucracies have to be staffed from somewhere, and no one is more mediocre than a well-taught student or an outstanding teacher.

19. Learning environments are not for everyone. As one student complained to me, "I am not paying my tuition to learn anything. I am paying for you to teach me something." Clearly, she had been taught a lot.

20. In one of my classes, I require participants to work on their examinations with at least one other person. They can work with as many others as they like. Even then, they don't have to work together on a single project. For example, Student X may write an essay, and Student Y may sing. Alternatively, they may collaborate on a single project, such as doing formal experimental research or writing a play. Regardless of the structure of the organization in which they elect to do their work, they have to share their grades.

21. The reason for the policy described in paragraph twenty may be found in my work and the works of Wilfred Bion (1961), James Lynch (1977), Rene Spitz (1946), and Dean Ornish (1998); all of us have pointed out that emotional connection with others is a requirement for survival. Consequently, any organizational policy, procedure, or action that requires people to work alone, in psychological isolation from one another, contributes to illness, both mental and physical (see Chapter Six).

22. The more I have learned to not*teach, the more I realize that connection with others is a requirement for survival, and the more I become interested in learning, the more I become enraged when people cheat. I define cheating as the failure to assist others on exams if they request it.

23. When I was a youngster and would moan and groan about not having anything to do, my grandfather would say, "Quit moping around and go learn yourself something." For a long time, I thought that his awkward use of the word *learn* indicated that he was both unlettered and not very bright. Now I realize that he may have been unlettered, but he sure as hell wasn't lacking in intellect.

24. I never read or discuss or pay attention to the data collected from the formal feedback systems that students and faculty frequently employ to evaluate faculty performance. Evidently such systems are useful to teachers, but they aren't useful to me. If I were to use those systems, I would be inviting both myself and my students to be taught the skills required to not*confront one another directly about our concerns and our delights as we attempt to work together. Ultimately, I would be teaching my students and myself how to develop the skills of passivity and non*risk-taking, which lead to interpersonal incompetence and irresponsibility when coping with human problems of organization. I am always willing to deal directly with my students about their compliments, concerns, or criticisms; but I have no interest in interrupting or breaking prayers or conducting training programs for organizational Sidestabbers (see Chapters Five and One).

25. The more I learn, the more I enjoy competence. The less I teach, the more I experience my own competence and the competence of others. I love to be around competent people, because I learn a lot from them, and I'm more competent in their presence.

26. The more I learn to not*teach, the more anxiety I experience in the classroom. I think my anxiety stems from the fact that I don't know what will happen from class session to class session and generally can't do much about what happens whenever it occurs.

27. Although I am more anxious in a learning environment, I also have a lot more fun. More events in the classroom are genuinely funny.

28. That reminds me: Have you ever wondered why textbooks aren't funny? Have you ever wondered why the Bible isn't funny? Probably because they were designed to teach you something.

29. Likewise, have you ever known a competent professor, preacher, politician, manager, employee, or student who *wasn't* funny, who *didn't* have a sense of humor or an appreciation of the absurd? I haven't. For example, did Jesus ever tell jokes or pass gas in church? He must have. (He drove the money changers out of the temple, didn't He?) When He did, I'll bet that the disciples roared and God laughed. I just wonder why His biographers forgot to tell us about it. Probably because they were trying to teach us something; but, by doing so, they destroyed part of His essence.

30. One last thought: if I've learned anything from being a university professor, it's that I try to teach only those whom I don't respect. And, God knows, if anything is in short supply in many contemporary organizations, it's a sense of shared respect.

Do let me know if you feel that I've tried to teach you something. If so, I will be glad to apologize.

CHAPTER FIVE

Prayers of Communication and Organizational Learning

Believing that the role of university faculty is to not*teach through the process of professing, I hereby profess, with more than a little fear and trembling, that prayer facilitates the development and maintenance of learning organizations.

I am aware that such professing may not be politically correct from the point of view of many who are engaged in organizational management, research, or consultation; so, in an effort to avoid needless misunderstandings, I think it might help if we agreed on some basic terminology. When I speak of *organizations,* I am referring to what Joseph Litterer (1969) described as "social units within which people have achieved somewhat stable relations (not necessarily face-to-face) in order to facilitate obtaining a set of objectives or goals." As for *learning organizations,* I borrow from the work of Karen Watkins and Victoria Marsik and define them as organizations that have the ability to transform themselves in ways that enhance their capacity for innovation and growth (1993).

I also profess that organizational learning can not occur efficiently, if at all, in a spiritual vacuum devoid of what Stephen Carter calls a presupposition of "the existence of a sentience beyond the human and capable of acting outside of the observed principles and limits of natural science" (1993, p. 17). That sentience frequently is expressed during day-to-day organizational life by the way in which we have prayerful relationships with others. In fact, whenever prayerful sentience is missing, organizational un*learning is rampant. (As discussed in Chapter Four, the asterisk indicates that the stem word is negated by its prefix and therefore describes an active process. Thus, we spend a lot of nonproductive, energy-draining, spirit-sapping energy engaging in activities such as organizational un*learning and dis*thinking.)

The fact that organizations engage in so much un*learning stemming from a failure to pray is why I believe members of all organizations, including families, churches, businesses, academic institutions, governmental agencies, and voluntary associations, must engage in prayer, particularly if they want to innovate and grow.

In the following pages, I discuss how I have concluded that prayer is important for organizational learning. Then I share some of my thoughts about the role of prayer in both learning and non*learning organizations. Those who worship at a Church of Transcendence might call my ruminations professions of faith. Those who place their faith in

How Come Every Time I Get Stabbed in the Back My Fingerprints Are on the Knife?

tenets of the Church of the Secular Scientist might describe them as working hypotheses. Those who find comfort in other professions of faith are welcome to invent appellations they find either more useful or more descriptive for them. As far as I'm concerned, the title of my thoughts is not important. Whatever you want to call them is all right with me.

Wellsprings of Prayerful Conclusions

I began to realize the important role that prayer plays in organizational learning several years ago during a conversation with Ronald Markillie, a close friend who describes himself as a psychoanalyst whose professional practice is an expression of his spiritual commitment. "Ron," I asked, "would you ever pray with a patient?"

"I don't know," he replied. "What do you have in mind?"

"Well, suppose you are working with a patient whose life is in shambles," I continued. "He is drinking heavily and his children are hooked on drugs. His wife, whom he loves dearly, is demanding a divorce. He is deeply in debt, and he has recently received notice that he is going to be fired by his longtime employer as part of a companywide downsizing program. He is in abject despair and crying. Suddenly he says, 'Dr. Markillie, I'm a religious person, and I know you are, too. Would you pray with me that God will see fit to lift these burdens from my shoulders?'"

Replied Ron, "Am I respecting how much the man is hurting? Am I respecting his suffering? Am I communicating my respect and concern for him as well as I know how?"

"Yes, Ron, you're doing all those good things."

A silence ensued. Then Ron continued, "By any chance is he trying to change the subject, to break the tension, to escape from the reality of the moment?"

"That's a peculiar question," I said. "Why do you ask?"

"Well," replied Ron, "sometimes when we get close to learning something important, I've noticed that we get frightened and try to escape by shifting the topic and running away to something that's easier to deal with."

"OK," I said, getting exasperated. "Let's say he is running. He *is* trying to escape. So what? Now's the time for you to quit trying to escape from answering my question. Would you pray with him?"

"Absolutely not."

"Why not?"

"It would interrupt the prayer we were having."

I didn't comprehend fully the meaning of Ron's response until several years later. I was a participant in a ten-person educational organization that had met at our church to discuss a book dealing with the loneliness Christ must have felt as he carried his cross to Calvary. About halfway through the time allocated for the meeting, Mr. Johnson (his name and the names of others have been changed to protect their privacy), our organization's eldest member, said, "Jesus must have been extremely lonely. Ever since my wife died, I have felt lonely much of the time, like I'm carrying a cross of my own."

When he concluded, a young woman, maybe one-third Mr. Johnson's age, replied, "Yes, Mr. Johnson, I think I know how that kind of loneliness feels. That's why I came here tonight—to try to keep from feeling lonely. Every now and then I feel so lonely, I just start to cry."

And she did.

As tears cascaded down her cheeks, she continued, "And when I get that way, I feel as if I don't want to live. Sometimes I think about killing myself. I've thought about killing myself all day. I started to do it, but then I remembered our meeting tonight and realized that I'd promised you I'd be here. I thought if I could meet with you, I might feel better."

A silence ensued. Had I measured its length by relying on the tightly wound inner clock that ticked behind my navel, I'd say the silence lasted at least an hour, maybe two. My trusty Timex contended that fifteen seconds expired. Regardless of its duration in clock time, the silence was heavy, suffocating, and, apparently, deafening. I know it was deafening because Deacon Conally, who was leading the discussion, said in a loud, chipper voice, full of vigor and infused with a tone of optimism, "Well, since all of us have a lot of things to do and nobody else has anything more to say, let's all stand, bow our heads, and close the meeting with a prayer."

When I described the event to one of my colleagues, Herb Koplowitz, he perceptively observed, "What Deacon Conally really said was, 'Let's close the prayer with a meeting.'"

Regardless of how one might describe our obvious effort to avoid confronting the reality of Mr. Johnson's loneliness, our young friend's contemplated suicide, and our collective terror by babbling panic-ridden double-talk to the Great CEO in the Sky, I immediately recalled my conversation with Ron Markillie. At that moment, I realized for the first time that engaging in caring, concerned, truth-seeking communication, suffused with a spirit of ineffable transcendence, is one important form of prayer. More important, I became aware that participation in such prayer is both a spiritual act and a requirement for organizational learning.

I also realized that the fragile Towers of Babel we construct from interrupted prayers, expressed in meaningless, fear-induced organizational double-talk, serve as metaphorical reminders of our alienation from one another—and from the Godhead. In addition, they prevent us from learning anything of significance in any organization; for who can engage in significant learning by participating in mindless, spiritless blather?

You might be interested to know, incidentally, that we didn't permanently destroy our prayer with the young woman, Mr. Johnson, and one another. Rather, one member of our organization found the spiritual courage to demand that we cease in our attempt to worship the totem created by our organizational gibberish. In fact, he insisted that we reengage ourselves in a prayerful conversation that ultimately provided us, individually and collectively, with a profound experience of organizational learning at its best.

Since having had those experiences of both non*prayer and prayer in a church organization—for which prayer is ostensibly integral to its stated mission (or, if you are a manager or organizational theorist, its mission statement)—

I have begun to call any caring, truth-seeking communication that is informed by a spirit of transcendence a *prayer of communication.*

With that definition in mind, I have since engaged in many such prayers with members of a wide variety of organizations about an enormously diverse set of topics. For example, I have prayed with others about their adventures with balance sheets and their adventures between bedsheets. I have prayed with others about engineering diagrams, organizational structures, and corporate visions. I have prayed with others about academic curricula, professional sports, family problems, and drinking problems. I have prayed in prose, poetry, song, and silence. I have prayed with others to the Godhead. You name the subject, and I have prayed with others to or about it in a wide variety of organizational environments.

To my regret, I also have interrupted and sometimes broken prayers of communication under equally diverse circumstances. As a general rule, when I have interrupted or broken a prayer of communication, I have felt damned lousy. That's not surprising to me. I suspect that feeling both damned and lousy is not unusual when we experience the alienation and isolation that inevitably stem from interrupting or breaking prayers of communication.

Given the range of my experiences with praying and with interrupting and breaking prayers of communication, I would like to share some of my ruminations about the essential nature of these prayers. In particular I would like to explore their relationship to the process of organizational learning and un*learning, realizing of course that my experiences with such prayers may not be yours. In fact, our different experiences might provide us with something of importance to pray about—together.

Ruminations About Prayers of Communication and Organizational Learning

1. Prayers of communication always involve an expression of Truth. Alternatively, interrupted prayers of communication involve the expression of Lies.

2. A lie is defined by Wilfred Bion—that great practitioner of psychoanalytic homiletics—not as a simple act of deceit but as "a formulation known by the initiator to be false, *but maintained as a barrier against statements that would otherwise lead to a psychological or emotional upheaval*" (Bion, 1970, p. 97, emphasis added). Had he said, "a psychological, emotional or *spiritual* upheaval," I believe he would have produced an extraordinary description of the experience one has when trying to avoid participating in a prayer of communication. He also would have provided a fecund hint as to why members of organizations frequently panic when confronted with the opportunity to engage in prayers of communication. Because of the upheaval that frequently emanates from its discovery, Truth is a paradoxical source of terror, spiritual development, and learning in organizational life.

3. Prayers of communication, being a spiritual activity devoted to the discovery and exploration of Truth, are unrelated to any particular religious persuasion, although they may be a part of any or none of them. In fact, since prayers of communication are requirements for organizational learning, whatever the context, one might argue that members of any organization who pray such prayers are spiritually engaged. Therefore, an individual participating in a prayer of communication might have spiritually based affiliations with any number of organizations, such as (but not restricted to) families, churches, businesses, voluntary associations, political parties, and athletic teams. I know that some of the most important prayer meetings I have attended revolved not around scriptures but around budgets.

4. Although members of all kinds of organizations can engage in prayers of communication, such prayers can't be employed to *promote* organizational learning. Prayers of communication have an existence and authenticity of their own. In the same way that Bion (1970) points out that thoughts exist independently of thinkers and that all we need for thoughts to exist is for someone to have the courage to think them, prayers of communication have an existence of their own: they just *are*. All we need for them to occur is for someone to pray them. However, if we try to employ, use, or manipulate them to achieve particular organizational goals—learning being one of them—they are destroyed. Attempting to use prayers to our advantage is as much an oxymoron as attempting to employ, use, or manipulate honesty, kindness, authenticity, decency, or humor for the same purpose. (Can't you just see a management training program on "How to Use Honesty to Get Your Way with Others"?)

5. Prayers of communication can't be part of an overall stratagem for organizational learning, either. They can't because a stratagem is, by definition, a "plan, scheme or trick for surprising or deceiving an enemy," or an "artifice, ruse or trick devised or used to attain a goal or to gain an advantage over an adversary or competitor, [an example being] business stratagems." Consequently, to assume that prayers of communication can be used to provide a climate for organizational learning, one would have to assume that organizational learning flourishes under conditions of ruses, deceptions, schemes, or tricks.

6. Because prayers of communication cannot be part of a stratagem, they can't have a strategic purpose either. They can't be employed to facilitate strategic planning, for example. In fact, if prayers of communication have a strategic purpose, they become interrupted prayers and avatars of organizational double-talk.

Maybe that's why members of the organization involved in the construction of the ancient Tower of Babel failed so miserably. Their strategy of "building a great city, with a temple-tower reaching to the skies—a proud eternal monument to themselves" disintegrated in chaos when the Gods "confused them by giving them many languages" (*The Living Bible: Paraphrased,* 1971, p. 8). Stated in the argot of contemporary organizations, their capacity to learn from and work with one another in a way that would permit the tower to be completed was destroyed. Unfortunately, the same dynamics described by the biblical myth-makers might summarize equally well the dynamics underlying the failure of strategic planning to facilitate organizational learning in many contemporary organizations.

7. If you accept Stephanie Marrus's contention (1984) that strategic planning involves long-range goals and that operational planning deals with the short-term, tactical maneuvers required to implement those goals, then prayers of communication can't be used for operational purposes either. When we attempt to engage in operational prayers, we only interrupt potentially longer prayers of communication at shorter intervals.

8. I've often wondered why so many messianic approaches that are meant to enhance organizational learning—such as management by objectives, total quality management, situational leadership, sensitivity training, zero-based budgeting, Managerial Grid Training,® and organizational development—have temporarily flourished and then entered into a state of decline. Since such efforts frequently involve stratagems for change, perhaps many of those associated with the targeted organization discovered that being participants in the artifices, ruses, and trickery inherent in any stratagem is spiritually debilitating. If that is true, such moribund approaches to organizational learning are fragile shards of interrupted or broken prayers that inhibit the very organizational learning they are designed to enhance. I just wonder why we apparently fear conducting the kind of organizational prayer meetings that would be required to facilitate their passing. May they rest in peace—or pieces.

9.   Some prayers of communication are not interrupted; they are irreparably broken. Like Humpty Dumpty, once broken, they can't be put together again. Those who have been estranged permanently from members of their families because of divorce, employees who have been cut off from their colleagues because of internal organizational fights or mass firings, or citizens who have been alienated from their countrymen because of political squabbles—all will understand the tragedies that accompany broken prayers.

10.   Since prayers of communication *are,* the capacity for engaging in them does not have to be learned, either individually or collectively. We are born with it. In the absence of a spiritual deficit (sometimes termed a neurosis or a psychosis) induced by a physiological infirmity or by participating in prolonged organizational un*learning, we maintain that capacity throughout our lives. Therefore, most members of any organization *have the capacity* to pray at any time; and it takes energy-draining not*praying for such organization members to not*engage in it. If an organization isn't learning, then, it is wasting a lot of energy and is ailing and spiritually infirm.

11.   Prayers to the Deity are another form of prayer, although I suppose that one might contend that since such

How Come Every Time I Get Stabbed in the Back My Fingerprints Are on the Knife?

prayers involve communication with the Godhead, they are ultimately prayers of communication.

Regardless of how organizational or religious theologians wish to categorize prayers to the Deity, I am impressed with how frequently such prayers play an important role in learning organizations. In my consulting practice, for instance, I frequently say to clients, "I am interested in your financial, marketing, engineering, sales, human resource, legal, and spiritual concerns. And, as part of the latter, I'm also interested in the way your prayer life (if any) may affect the way you work." Under those conditions, many of them engage in prayers of communication with me about their prayers to the Deity. Furthermore, I nearly always get a ride to the airport from someone who wants to continue our prayer for as long as possible.

Consistent with the thesis propounded by Stephen Carter in *The Culture of Disbelief* (1993), most members of ostensibly secular organizations, particularly formal organizations, apparently believe that admitting to conversing with the Godhead about organizational problems is inappropriate. They fear that such admissions of "God-talk" will destroy their careers despite the fact that in countries such as the United States, "nine out of ten . . . believe in God and four out of five pray regularly" (p. 4).

For example, I find that CEOs are very hesitant to inform their boards of directors that they have decided to invest millions of dollars, not because of their systematic interpretations of engineering, financial, and marketing data but because they prayed to the Deity and the Deity encouraged them to do it. Likewise, many professionals in my field, including those who take great pride in being dispassionate scientists in search of Truth, are so terrified when (or if) their clients want to discuss the Truth of their prayer lives that they panic, interrupt, and, in many cases, break their clients' attempts at prayer rather than participate in them. For reasons unclear to me, I think that most of us in my profession find it more comfortable to deal with the intricacies of secular ego defenses or double-loop learning. (For a discussion of double-loop learning, see Argyris and Schon, 1978.) Doing so is easier than exploring the impact that "a sentience beyond the human and capable of acting outside of the observed principles and limits of natural science" (Carter, 1993, p. 17) has on the way in which organizational learning takes place.

If you don't believe me, ask yourself how many behavioral scientists have produced articles, monographs, and books that deal with the effect of prayers to the Deity on the functioning of learning organizations. If you know of any, please call me, collect.

12. Maybe managers, organizational development consultants, organizational theorists, and behavioral science researchers will someday develop the courage to overcome their fear of the psychological and spiritual upheaval that occurs within them when they are offered the opportunity to prayerfully explore the way in which prayers to the Deity actually affect not only organizational learning but organizational functioning in general.

How Come Every Time I Get Stabbed in the Back My Fingerprints Are on the Knife?

If Bion is correct, overcoming that fear requires that we give up our preference for promulgating organizational lying and the dis*learning that inevitably accompanies it.

13. Having gained a new understanding of prayers of communication, I understand better the meaning of the term *communing with nature*. At one time I thought communing with nature was primarily an excuse employed by New Age zealots when police apprehended them for gamboling nude in public parks. Now I realize that it's more likely a description of a spiritual process that facilitates organizational learning in *very* complex organizations. It's probably the process Eugene Mallove attempted to describe when he discussed the puzzling spirituality integral to "Einstein's intoxication with the God of the Cosmos" (1985, p. C4).

14. Perhaps such large-scale prayers of communication are what Czech president Vaclav Havel had in mind during his Declaration of Interdependence. As only a poet could, he reminded us that "all human beings are mysteriously connected to the universe," that "we are not here alone nor for ourselves alone, but . . . are an integral part of higher, mysterious entities against whom it is not advisable to blaspheme," and that self-transcendence, which touches the depth of our lives, is a requirement for learning to engage in the type of international collaboration required to facilitate our planet's survival (cited in Scenitz, 1994, p. 66).

15. "They don't have a prayer." In case you are unfamiliar with the phrase, it means that the subjects of the thought are inextricably enmeshed in circumstances that will result in their injury or destruction. For instance, "When the CEO announced his opposition to his subordinates' plan, they didn't have a prayer of getting it accepted," or "When the troops were surrounded, they didn't have a prayer of escaping."

The subjects of the phrase may face an infinite number of problems, but when it comes to learning whatever is required for innovation and growth within an organization, I am convinced that those who don't pray don't have a prayer.

16. According to Joseph Campbell, "if you do follow your bliss you put yourself on a kind of track that has been there all the while, waiting for you, and the life that you ought to be living is the one you are living. . . . Wherever you are—if you are following your bliss, you are enjoying that refreshment, that life within you, all the time" (Campbell and Moyers, 1988, p. 150). Until recently, I never thought I understood what he was talking about, particularly in regard to day-to-day organizational life.

Now I suspect that "following your bliss" is the outcome of engaging in prayers of communication within organizations of which we are a part, and not*following it is both a cause and an effect of interrupted or broken prayers. Knowing that you have a bliss and not being able to find it must be a source of both personal misery and organizational dysfunction, and living in an organization that encourages you to not*learn to find your bliss must be sheer hell.

17. Any organizational policy, procedure, system, structure, or action that consistently interrupts or breaks prayers of communication generates anaclitic depression. For those who may not be familiar with it, anaclitic depression is a form of illness-producing, and sometimes life-threatening, depression we frequently suffer when we are separated from or abandoned by individuals, organizations, or ideas we rely on for emotional support. (For a discussion of the impact of anaclitic depression on organizational functioning, see Chapter Six.)

Thus, when we threaten one another's security by downsizing, we destroy the spiritual climate required for prayers of communication and organizational learning. When we appraise one another's performances within the theoretical constraints of a bell-shaped curve, thereby implicitly saying, "If someone else in the organization does well, your probability of doing well is decreased," the likelihood that we will pray with and learn from one another in the organization is also decreased. When we introduce new ideas in ways that destroy the sense of connection and security that the old ways of living and working provided, the probability that we will pray with and learn from one another is lessened. Regardless of the circumstances, whenever organizational dynamics of our own construction encourage or require that we interrupt or break prayers of communication, the probability increases that we will suffer the alienation, separation, or abandonment that generates anaclitic depression.

18. If you want some concrete and very creative information on how to structure formal hierarchical organizations that by their nature reduce anaclitic depression, facilitate prayers of communication, and enhance organizational learning, read *Requisite Organization* by Elliott Jaques (1989). In essence, Jaques contends that any organization will function much more effectively if all organizational members are held accountable by leaders who possess greater intellectual capability than they.

Should you decide to read the book, you may have difficulty finishing it. As I point out in Chapter Eight, Jaques's work frequently creates a lot of upheaval in those who attempt to comprehend it. When that happens, they tend to interrupt their prayer with the author and encourage others to do the same. Assuming Bion is correct when he asserts that truthful formulations frequently generate a lot more turmoil than lies, Jaques's book must contain a lot of truth . . . and that's no lie.

19. I often engage in prayers of communication with members of organizations to which I belong. Maybe such prayers reflect a spiritual odyssey similar to the one described by Isaac Bashevis Singer when he said, "Whenever I am in trouble, I pray, and since I'm always in trouble, I pray a lot. Even when you see me eat and drink, while I do this, I pray" (cited in Barrett, 1979, p. 308). Unfortunately, because of barriers in my spirit—barriers created

How Come Every Time I Get Stabbed in the Back My Fingerprints Are on the Knife?

by informal norms and barriers created by bizarre man-made social structures in the organizations to which I belong—I sometimes don't pray with members of my organizations. As a result, I fail to take advantage of many learning opportunities that occur in organizations where I reside but, at times, don't live and occasionally die—even while breathing.

20. All prayers of communication, regardless of the organization in which they occur, are expressions of that which is spiritual and sacred. Consequently, learning anything of significance in any organization requires that we permit ourselves to experience that which most of us refer to as God. For significant organizational learning to occur, then, we must have transcendent visions that extend far beyond our worship of the bottom line or the efficient production of nails.

21. Do you believe that?

22. If not, I would never attempt to convince you that my profession (or any other profession I have made) is valid; for to do so would require that I interrupt—or break—what for me has been a prayer.

CHAPTER SIX

This Is a Football:
Leadership and the
Anaclitic Depression
Blues

You probably know a lot about the theory and practice of leadership. I suspect, however, that you aren't sated with information regarding the anaclitic depression blues and the way in which it interferes with our capacity to serve as leaders.[1] I know that I haven't found it to be a common topic of conversation at management seminars or cocktail parties, at least not the ones I attend, anyway.

If my suspicion is correct, I imagine I am in a position similar to the one in which Vince Lombardi, the famous football coach, found himself immediately after his beloved Green Bay Packers had played an extremely poor game. According to the story I heard, Lombardi stormed into the team's dressing room after the game and, in a fury that only he could generate, shouted at the players: "Don't even bother taking your uniforms off. As soon as the stands clear, we are going back on the field and practice. I don't care if it is sixty-eight degrees below zero and it takes us until four-thirty tomorrow morning. We are going to stay out there until we learn to play this game correctly. We are going to start with the fundamentals and work up from there." Still seething, he grabbed a football from a nearby ball basket and held it up before his absolutely hushed audience. "Here is where we begin. This, gentlemen, is a football."

There was a forty-second silence. Then Max McGee, a player better known for his devil-may-care attitude than his athletic talent, said, "Will you go over that again, Coach?" (For another version, see Kramer, 1970, p. 129.)

Like Coach Lombardi, I want to focus on the basics and explore one of the fundamentals that underlie many of the ideas that I develop in this book. To accomplish that goal, I plan to not*teach about the anaclitic depression blues. I will hold "the blues" up for your inspection. Like Lombardi's football, it is at the essence of the "game" I am playing as I explore the mysteries of organizational life in general and leadership behavior in particular. Who knows? It might turn out to be suitable material to kick around at management seminars and cocktail parties to which you are invited.

Reviewing the Rules

Given the importance of both leadership and anaclitic depression to my meditations, I will commence my locker-room oration by defining both terms to ensure that we are playing by the same set of rules. In the absence of shared definitions, what one person terms a football, another may

How Come Every Time I Get Stabbed in the Back My Fingerprints Are on the Knife?

call a posterior. Confusing the two can have painful consequences, particularly if the posterior belongs to you.

Next I discuss how the anaclitic depression blues finds expression in individual, organizational, and conceptual playing fields. Then I explore the relationship of anaclitic depression to the well-known pseudophenomenon "resistance to change." Finally, I set forth a major generalization about the relationship between anaclitic depression and the process of leadership. That generalization will serve as a segue into the subsequent chapter, "What If I Really Believe This Stuff?"

The Process of Leadership

When I speak of leadership, I am describing what Elliott Jaques and Steve Clement call "that process in which one person sets the purpose or direction for one or more others and gets them to move along with him or her and with each other in that direction with competence and full commitment" (Jaques and Clement, 1991, p. 4). Leadership, so defined, is expressed in a wide array of organizational roles—managerial leadership, pastoral leadership, professorial leadership, parental leadership, political leadership, military leadership, anarchic leadership, and an infinite variety of other types of leadership, depending on your role in a particular organization. Since leadership is grounded in the organizational role you play, you don't have to waste precious time and energy engaging in dreary debates about whether managers, parents, coaches, politicians, members of the military, professors, priests, poets, or anarchists are leaders. They are leaders if they carry out the defined process of leadership within the framework of an organizational role.

This definition of leadership, I hope you realize, requires that you, the leader, be emotionally bonded, attached, connected, or linked with those whom you lead. It also requires that those whom you lead be emotionally bonded, attached, connected, or linked with you and with one another. That's what shared purpose and commitment are all about. In the absence of those emotional bonds, individuals in leadership roles are unable to exert the type of influence that is required for them to lead. They may coerce potential followers to comply with their desires by employing a wide range of organizational rewards and sanctions that go with the authority of their offices, but such actions have nothing to do with leadership. True leadership manifests itself only in volitional relationships between and among leaders and followers. That is why I am convinced that the anaclitic depression blues is so relevant to the leadership process.

Anaclitic Depression

Anaclitic comes from the Greek word *anaclisis,* which means "to lean upon." *Anaclitic depression,* therefore, is the term I use to describe a particular, circumscribed form of melancholia that we often experience when the individuals, organizations, or belief systems that we lean on or are dependent on for emotional support are withdrawn from us. For instance, when we are "put down" by someone in a leadership role or jilted by a lover, or when we go through the trials and tribulations of an organizational downsizing, suffer through a corporate reorganization over which we have no control, or have to relinquish a cherished belief system, we often suffer from the ravages of the anaclitic depression blues.[2]

Unabated, anaclitic depression may culminate in *marasmus,* which means "to waste away." In early usage, marasmus meant "to quench, as fire; pass; to die away." Given its historical definition, I find that marasmus is a particularly apt term for describing what happens to many organization members when they are downsized, outplaced, or RIFed (that is, when they lose their jobs due to a "reduction in force"). Listen to how they discuss their lives with one another. They consistently describe themselves as being consumed by the experience of getting fired—as being burned out, parched, enervated, withered, or weakened by the event. Etymology, at times, has a very utilitarian function.

Anaclitic Depression in Infancy

Anaclitic depression was identified approximately fifty years ago by Rene Spitz (1946) during his observations of infants in a foundling home. The infants received adequate food, clothing, and medical care. However, because the home was understaffed, these infants rarely were picked up, played with, stroked, or given loving support and attention by their harried caretakers. Under those conditions of what mental health professionals call separation or maternal deprivation, many of the infants became lethargic, tense, and fearful. They frequently refused to eat, had difficulty sleeping, and cried a lot more than comparable infants who had their emotional needs met by supportive adults. Eventually, even when adults appeared on the scene, the infants withdrew into their "shells." They became marasmic, losing weight and wasting away physically. As anaclitic depression progressed, some developed vacant, faraway looks in their eyes similar to the ones seen in many individuals as they approach death. Ultimately, and inexplicably to the well-meaning adults who cared for them, approximately one-third of the infants died.

In follow-up studies by Spitz and others, researchers have found that virtually all infants who suffer anaclitic depression, even those who survive it, incur some degree of permanent impairment in physical, social, and intellectual development. From this research, it is clear that to survive and thrive, infants require attachment, "an affectionate bond between two individuals that endures through space and time and serves to join them emotionally" (Kennell, Voos, and Klaus, 1976, p. 25).

The absence of an affectionate bond or emotional linkage with an "attachment figure" during infancy is associated with other problems as well. For instance, in *High Risk: Children Without a Conscience*, Ken Magid and Carole McKelvey (1987) report that infants who suffer "attachment disorders" tend to develop a broad range of emotional problems that recur throughout their lifetimes. As they pass from infancy to childhood and then to adulthood, their ability to "make and maintain affectional bonds is always disordered" (Bowlby, 1979, p. 72).

If you carry that simple statement to its logical conclusion, many such emotionally injured individuals will have difficulty both getting and staying married because they won't be able to make the emotional commitment that marriage requires. They will have difficulty holding jobs because they won't be able to make the emotional commitment—which in organizational terms is described as loyalty—that extended employment requires. And as Magid and McKelvey point out, when emotionally injured infants become children, teenagers, and adults, a disproportionate number of them become physically brutal and dangerous in their relationships with others. In the worst-case scenarios, they do not develop a sense of conscience, remorse, or guilt and frequently become the individuals who—at age eleven or sixteen or forty-six—meander down the streets of your hometown armed with a .38 and take someone's life with no apparent concern about what they have done. Have you noticed how often that occurs these days?

Anaclitic Depression Beyond Infancy

In the psychiatric community, anaclitic depression is considered to be a disorder that affects only infants, although it is recognized to have a variety of negative consequences later in life. A lot of persuasive evidence exists, however, that children, teenagers, adults, and the elderly have the same strong need for affectionate emotional bonds with others in order to survive and thrive. The destruction of these bonds frequently results in essentially the same type of dysfunctional consequences that befall infants who suffer from the anaclitic depression blues.

For instance, when you were a child, were you abandoned by one or both of your parents because of death, divorce, or adoption? According to John Bowlby (1969, pp. xiii-xiv), the author of *Attachment and Loss,*

> loss of [a] mother-figure, either by itself or in combination with other variables yet to be clearly identified, is capable of generating responses and processes that are . . . the very same known to be active in older individuals who are still disturbed by separations they suffered early in life. Amongst these responses and processes and amongst forms of disturbances are, on the one hand, a tendency to make excessive demands and to be anxious and angry when they are not met, such as is present in dependent and hysterical personalities; and on the other, a blockage in the capacity to make deep relationships such as is present in affectionate-less and psychopathic relationships.

In the language of everyday living, Bowlby means that if your coworkers, friends, or family members make inordinate, insatiable demands on you for support and reassurance, it may be that they have suffered from the anaclitic depression blues as infants or children. Likewise, if you have family members, friends, or coworkers who consistently fly off the handle because of imagined slights (such as not being invited to business meetings or social events that they have no legitimate reason to attend), they may

116

well have been injured by the anaclitic depression blues early in life. The same is true for your witty, charming, unmarried Uncle Elrod, who has a long history of panicking and heading for the hills every time his significant other hints that she wants to tie the knot.

Speaking of tying the knot, did your parents untie the knot by getting divorced when you were a child? If they did, when compared with people whose parents did not divorce, you are more likely to have had poor relationships with both them and your own children, to have exhibited problem behavior, to have dropped out of high school, and to have required professional psychological help (Zill, Morrison, and Coiro, 1993). You will probably have entered school with significantly less social and academic competence than your two-parent peers (Guidubaldi and Perry, 1984). You are more likely to have failed a grade and to have suffered from a variety of other forms of emotional distress, including depression, impulsiveness, and destructiveness, than children whose parents did not divorce (Wood and others, 1993). Feeling that we have been divorced by our parents contributes to the anaclitic depression blues and, for many of us, results in life experiences about which we do not have fond memories.

In case the preceding information has not depressed you sufficiently, would you like another example of the way in which you are affected beyond infancy and childhood by your early relationships with your parents? Well, supposing that you were a male college student in the early 1950s; if you said that you had "very close" or "warm and friendly" relationships with your parents, by midlife you would have an approximately 50 percent chance of having a serious chronic disease. In contrast, if you said that your relationships with your parents were "tolerant" or "strained and cold," your probability of having a serious chronic illness by middle age would approach 100 percent (Ornish, 1998).

The experience of separation frequently has a dramatic impact on parents, as well. For instance, have you recently sent your only, or last, child away to college or had that child engage in the rites of holy matrimony? If you and your child have participated in either (or both) of those events, you might want to know that representatives of the Kodak Company interviewed the next of kin of twenty-six employees who died suddenly from coronary disease and found that "common to at least fifty percent of the sudden deaths was the departure of the last or only child in the family for college or marriage, in response to which the parent had been depressed" (Lynch, 1977, p. 61). I suspect that this mortality rate applies even if the parents had looked forward to the peace and quiet that supposedly accompanies roosting in an empty nest.

During World War II, anaclitic depression was a significant contributor, in both children and adults, to what was called Mussulmans Syndrome. The syndrome received its imposing appellation because individuals who suffered from it frequently assumed a modified fetal position, which from a distance appeared to be very similar to the posture adopted by Moslems when they are engaged in prayer— on their knees with foreheads touching the floor.

Mussulmans Syndrome was originally identified in inmates of concentration camps. Under those extremely arduous conditions, individuals who were separated suddenly from their families and loved ones frequently "gave way to profound despair, lost hope and perished" (Lynch, 1977, p. 123). Although one could never argue that the state of prevailing physical deprivation was similar, Lynch's description of the outcome of sudden separation in the camps is very close to Spitz's description of what occurred to anaclitically depressed infants in the orphanage. Clearly, all of us, infants or not, require supportive emotional attachment both to live and to thrive, regardless of the physical environments in which we reside.

Similarly, Captain Eugene McDaniel, who was a POW in North Vietnam, reported that the probability of POWs' dying in captivity increased if they were unable to give and receive emotional support by communicating with one another. As he explained in *Scars and Stripes,* his captors "knew, as well as I and the others did, that a man could stand more pain if he is *linked* with others. . . . The lone, isolated being becomes weak, vulnerable. I knew I had to make contact, no matter what the cost" (McDaniel, with Johnson, 1975, p. 40, emphasis added).

Again, we find that attachment to others, like oxygen, is a requirement for our health and survival. This is true regardless of our age, gender, political affiliation, educational level, religious background, or national origin. The broken heart is not a romanticized figment of some dewy-eyed, woebegone poet's imagination. It is very real.

If you want to learn more about the linkage between separation and health problems associated with the anaclitic depression blues, read *The Broken Heart: The Medical Consequences of Loneliness,* by James Lynch (1977), or *Love and Survival,* by Dean Ornish (1998). According to the research reported by both Lynch and Ornish, loneliness is a major contributor to premature death from heart disease and to a variety of other major illnesses.

Loneliness is a common, everyday word that we spontaneously employ to describe the feeling we have when we are suffering from anaclitic depression. Consequently, when you, your coworkers, spouse, children, peers, bosses, friends, or enemies complain of feeling lonely, either you or they are probably experiencing the anaclitic depression blues. Listen carefully to yourself and to the people around you, particularly those with whom you work. I think you will be surprised at how often we speak of loneliness, which indicates, I think, the central role that the anaclitic depression blues plays in our day-to-day organizational lives.

Lynch's and Ornish's data about the relationship between death rates and attachment to others are compelling. For example, whether you are married, single, divorced, or "looking," you might want to contemplate the following information: "At all ages, for both sexes and for all races in the United States, the non-marrieds always have higher death rates, sometimes as much as five times higher than those of married individuals" (Lynch, 1977, p. 52).

You can interpret these data in a variety of ways. The interpretation that Lynch, Ornish, and I prefer is that being

How Come Every Time I Get Stabbed in the Back My Fingerprints Are on the Knife?

emotionally linked through marriage reduces the probability that we will suffer from the pervasive loneliness that I characterize as the anaclitic depression blues. Furthermore, if we are lonely, our probability of departing from this world prematurely is higher than if we have secure, comfort-providing attachments with others who assuage our sense of psychological isolation.

Not everyone agrees with this interpretation. For example, one of my friends responded, "You guys have missed the point entirely. The data say that you can live longer in hell or you can die young while enjoying yourself." Regardless of your interpretation, I would not go out of my way to sell you a life insurance policy unless you possess a valid marriage license.

Although the death rates for both men and women are lower when their loneliness is assuaged by marriage, who do you think marriage favors the most: men or women?[3] If you said "men," you are correct. There is a greater difference in mortality risk between married and unmarried men than there is between married and unmarried women.[4] Men also tend to suffer from the throes of divorce more than women. For instance, if you are a divorced male, your probability of dying from a coronary is 2.08 times that of married males; but if you are a divorced female your probability is only 1.40 times that of married females (Lynch, 1977). Furthermore, widowed males have proportionally higher death rates than widowed females, and single males have proportionally higher death rates than single females (Lynch, 1977; Shurtleff, 1956). Although the broken heart

is not a figment of the poet's imagination, the poet's imagination apparently is stimulated more by observing lonely
men than by observing lonely women.

In consideration of the preceding data, I can't help but
conclude that where reactions to anaclitic depression in organizations are concerned, men and women do differ.
Therefore, if you occupy an organizational leadership role,
you had better take those differences into account. One
might even say that, in the realm of anaclitic depression,
God has played a sexist joke—on men.

Abandonment by Organizations

Being abandoned by, ostracized by, or separated from individuals whom we know and lean on is an experience
that frequently has a devastating impact on our lives. Likewise, being ostracized by, separated from, or abandoned
by cherished organizations, many of whose members we
may not know personally, can generate the anaclitic depression blues.

For instance, consider the recent rash of organizational
events we euphemistically term *downsizings, reductions in
force, rightsizings, strategic personnel realignments, reengi-
neerings, disestablishments,* and *outplacements* that plague
employees of contemporary formal organizations. We don't
employ those euphemisms by accident. We use them so
that we won't have to cope with the misery of being aware

How Come Every Time I Get Stabbed in the Back My Fingerprints Are on the Knife?

that firing people from their jobs ultimately means discharging them from the organization as we would fire a bullet from a pistol or an artillery shell from a howitzer (see Barnhart, 1995).

Regardless of the euphemisms we employ in an effort to assuage the guilt we frequently feel for designing or implementing such events, firing innocent people from their organizations as if we were firing them from guns frequently creates the anaclitic depression blues. Consequently, when members of a formal organization fire their friends, enemies, and colleagues from the organization like cannonballs, you know in advance that many of those *involved* in the firing, including those who are not fired, suffer from feelings of separation and abandonment followed by the anaclitic depression blues. I don't understand how we could expect otherwise.

We also tend to refer to our rejection of others under those circumstances as axing, cutting, slicing, or chopping them; and we know that they will bleed. The anaclitic depression blues that accompanies these debilitating injuries, injuries that are inflicted by ostensible friends and colleagues, frequently scars them forever. Covered with scar tissue, these individuals inevitably serve as visible reminders of what could happen to those who remain.

The progression of the anaclitic depression blues that results from participating in the organizationally sanctioned process of separating, abandoning, or ostracizing innocent souls who lean on us for emotional support is very similar to the process identified by Kübler-Ross (1997) in her description of our preparation for death, the ultimate separation experience. From my observations, I have found that the progression includes the following phases. Phase I consists of anger directed toward the organization. In Phase II, the anger is reversed and focused inward, creating depression. In Phase III, the person sinks into apathy, which is depression dispersed and spread about. In this phase, people frequently have difficulty getting out of their beds in the morning; if they succeed, they often head for their couches and lifelessly glue their eyes to "the tube" for hours at a time. The process concludes with Phase IV, detachment, which is depression transformed into scar tissue that covers an unhealed—and now unhealable—wound. Once people have reached the detachment stage, the organization can rehire their bodies, but it can't resuscitate the souls that gave those bodies life.

Like Spitz's infants, the people who reach the detachment stage are permanently damaged. They will never work for the organization that fired them, or for any other formal organization for that matter, with the same sense of enthusiasm, loyalty, and commitment they had before they were separated from and abandoned by people on whom they leaned, not only for their livelihoods but also for their emotional well-being and, sometimes, even for their lives.

If you don't believe my assertion, think about individuals you know who lost their jobs in the Great Depression of the 1930s. For many of them, it should have been called the Great Anaclitic Depression because the impact of the blues that accompanied the Depression affected them for the remainder of their lives. Although they may have been

124

employed for many years after the Depression, those who had reached the detachment stage frequently showed up at their places of employment with "one foot out the door" and "mad money in the cookie jar." Furthermore, when they returned to their homes in the evening, they warned their children never to trust their employers to take care of them when "the going gets tough." My father and mother certainly did that. Perhaps your parents and grandparents did, too.

For me, the ultimate tragedy of firing innocent people stems not from what it does to their pocketbooks but from the manner in which the anaclitic depression blues withers their souls.

When I said that a lot of those involved in the process of downsizing develop the anaclitic depression blues, I did not use the word *involved* by chance. When organization members fire one another out the door, many of those who are not fired but who remain as unexpended—but clearly expendable—ammunition also suffer from the anaclitic depression blues. It is called Layoff Survivor's Sickness (Noer, 1993), a term derived from Survivor's Syndrome, which describes the depression, guilt, and spiritual marasmus experienced both by survivors of the Nazi Holocaust and by Japanese survivors of the atomic explosions at Hiroshima and Nagasaki (Lifton, 1986).

The impact of Layoff Survivor's Sickness is elucidated in detail by David Noer in *Healing the Wounds* (1993). According to Noer, it is a combination of stress, fatigue, decreased motivation, sadness, depression, insecurity, anxiety, fear, decreased loyalty to the organization, numbness, and resignation that frequently plagues those who are *not* fired when an organization downsizes. Having observed that Layoff Survivor's Sickness persisted for five years after a downsizing in the very large organization he studied, Noer concluded, "Time, it would appear, does not heal all wounds" (p. 71).

Damn. If I didn't know that I was reading about the long-term impact of separation-induced anaclitic depression on adults who were abandoned by their organization, I would think I was reading the results of Rene Spitz's work with infants who were abandoned by their primary "attachment figures." The symptoms are virtually identical.

Perhaps I was. If our mommies, metaphorical or actual, abandon or ostracize us, it doesn't make any difference whether we are adults or infants. We apparently suffer in much the same way. Ma Bell, the benevolent organization that was well known not for being "lean and mean" but for the long-term emotional security she provided for her employees, was not called Ma Bell without reason.

Stated differently, when our bosses, colleagues, and subordinates (many of whom are strangers to us), acting on behalf of an organization upon which we lean for life-giving emotional support, withdraw that support from us, most of us behave like infants again. Or one might even say, with more than slight justification, that Spitz's infants, once they had been separated from their families, suddenly and inexplicably began to behave like adults who have been involuntarily separated from their employer.

On the offhand chance that you are detail oriented and need numbers to describe the relationship between the anaclitic depression blues and job loss, Merva and Fowles (1993) report that for every 1 percent increase in unemployment, deaths from heart disease increase 6 percent, deaths from stroke increase 3 percent, and homicides increase 7 percent. To me, the statistics are quite sterile; the body counts are not.

In addition to directing downsizings, individuals in leadership roles frequently engage in creating, or collude to produce, a virtually endless variety of other common organizational procedures, policies, and structures that generate the anaclitic depression blues. The following paragraphs describe a few:

1. Failing to provide job or employment security. *Job security* means that you can rely on your linkage with your employer to provide secure employment. *Employment security* means that you can rely on the political process to facilitate your finding linkage with others through employment—if you want it—at your level of capability. Involuntary unemployment, when it results in anaclitic depression, breaks the emotional bonds that bind individuals, organizations, and political systems together and thereby compromises the ability of individuals in leadership roles to lead.

2. Requiring organizational members to participate in involuntary reorganizations over which they have no control. Frequently, doing so demands that followers break emotional linkages with their leaders, friends, colleagues, and ways of working that provide them with the emotional security required to protect themselves against the ravages of anaclitic depression blues.

3. Conducting performance appraisals based on the underlying premise that the distribution of individual performance in organizations matches a bell-shaped curve. By employing that premise the leader is saying, "If someone else in the organization does well, your probability of doing well is decreased." It therefore becomes important for coworkers to avoid developing close relationships with one another, because under such a system, each person ultimately is rewarded for "doing the other in" (Harvey, 1993, p. 94). In that environment of forced psychological isolation, the anaclitic depression blues throws the organization for major losses, as Coach Lombardi might say.

4. Structuring the organization so that subordinates are held accountable for their work by people in managerial leadership roles who are less capable than the people whom they ostensibly manage (Jaques, 1989). As my colleague Elliott Jaques so clearly demonstrates, the anger, frustration, distrust, and paranoia that attends such a reporting relationship frequently creates the sense of separation and abandonment that results in the anaclitic depression blues. The blues, in turn, destroys the emotional linkages that are required for leaders to gain the sense of shared purpose and commitment that is required for the exercise of effective leadership.

128

5. Establishing unfair differentials between the compensation of those at the top and those at the bottom of the organization. Angry controversies are raging over the fact that CEOs of U.S. Fortune 500 companies receive compensation that averages thirty-five times—and, in some cases, one thousand times—that of their average manufacturing employees, whereas in comparable European organizations the differential is twenty and in Japanese organizations, fifteen (Nelson-Horchler, 1990). The anger that accompanies the recognition of differentials that are perceived as unfair generates a sense of emotional separation between the leaders and their followers. That separation, again, generates anaclitic depression and destroys the emotional linkages required for the competent exercise of managerial leadership.

6. Failing to provide both formal and informal organizational procedures that facilitate forgiving one another for mistakes. As I described in "Captain Asoh and the Concept of Grace" (1988c), providing mechanisms for organizational grace—defined as "unmerited forgiveness"—is a requirement for reconciling otherwise fractured emotional relationships between and among organization members. Fractured relationships frequently lead to the anaclitic depression blues. For instance, if a record of your mistakes goes into your permanent personnel file so that you can be held eternally accountable for your past incompetent actions and errors of judgment, anaclitic depression is likely to follow.

The number of ways in which individuals in organizational leadership roles contribute to creating the anaclitic depression blues in themselves and others is, for all practical purposes, endless. However, like Coach Lombardi when he hoisted the football for a quick inspection by members of his team, I am interested only in discussing the fundamentals of the game. I am not interested in reviewing its manifold nuances.

Abandonment by Theories, Ideas, and Belief Systems

Finally, we frequently suffer anaclitic depression when we are involuntarily separated from ideas, theories, and belief systems on which we have leaned for emotional security and comfort. Paradoxically, where ideas, theories, and belief systems are involved, the suffering that stems from the anaclitic depression blues is seldom expressed directly. Rather, it is manifest in our attempts *to avoid* the suffering. That thought is not unique. Wilfred Bion, for one, pointed out that the fear, anxiety, and depression that invariably accompany learning something new and important cause us to resist both the idea and its proponents in an effort to avoid an intense emotional upheaval (Symington and Symington, 1997). I call that upheaval the anaclitic depression blues.

For instance, citizens in the Western world did not shout hosannas when Galileo provided scientific verifica-

How Come Every Time I Get Stabbed in the Back My Fingerprints Are on the Knife?

tion of Copernicus's theory that the earth revolves around the sun, not vice versa. In an effort to circumvent the anaclitic depression that threatened them when they considered abandoning their comfortable belief system and accepting a fundamentally different view of humanity's place in the universe, officials of the Church brought Galileo before an Inquisition. They convicted him, required him to recant, and placed him under long-term house arrest to ensure that he wouldn't threaten them with the blues again.

The medical establishment was not overwhelmed with joy when Dr. Ignaz Semmelweiss reported, in 1860, that deaths from childbed fever could be reduced from 12 percent to less than 1 percent if, when delivering a baby, physicians would wash their hands in a weak solution of chlorine and ensure that childbirth took place in a clean room on clean bedsheets. To accept that point of view would have required that physicians abandon the comfortable belief, long promulgated in medical textbooks and training, that childbed fever was caused by an "invisible miasm . . . of an atmospheric-cosmic-telluric nature" (de Kruif, 1932, p. 39).

Faced with the fear of suffering the anaclitic depression blues if they accepted Semmelweiss's revolutionary new approach to the practice of obstetrics, the medical establishment chose to fight him tooth and nail. Apparently, they sought to protect themselves from having to give up not only a complex of related ideas on which they leaned for emotional support but also their association with an isomorphic network of medical societies, training programs, interpersonal alliances, political coalitions, and other collateral social and belief systems that were associated with the idea.

Creationists were not bathed in ecstasy when Darwin published his thesis that the process of evolution, not the antics of Adam and Eve, produced the human species. In fact, they placed a young school teacher, John Scopes, on trial and convicted him for teaching Darwinism in the Tennessee public schools. They, too, apparently sought to avoid the anaclitic depression blues that they feared would follow if they abandoned a cherished religious belief system from which they had long derived comfort, security, and reassurance.

Anaclitic Depression and Resistance to Change

From the preceding three examples, many people might stoutly contend that the Church, the medical establishment, and the creationists, like most people with limited insight and moral courage, were resistant to change. I don't accept that explanation. In fact, because of the regularity with which we respond fearfully to being abandoned by individuals and organizations or to being forced to accept new belief systems, I have concluded that, regardless of its context, what most of us refer to as resistance to change is not resistance to change at all. Rather, it is the resistance to par-

132

ticipating in experiences of separation, alienation, or loss, any of which can lead to the anaclitic depression blues.

If you don't believe me, look at the way the term *resistance to change* is used in everyday life. First, it is generally employed by those who do not expect to suffer from anaclitic depression because of a change they want to introduce, a change that probably will cause anaclitic depression in others. Simultaneously, these people use the term to justify their taking punitive action against those who do not fully cooperate with the change. In that sense, use of the term becomes a scientifically justified and subtlety sophisticated approach to blaming the victim. For instance, someone who fancies himself as a "change agent" might stoutly contend that "Joan is fighting my reengineered organizational structure [that will cause her to lose her job, give up many of her friends and colleagues, abandon the standard of living to which she is accustomed, and quit using a cherished skill that has taken her years to develop]. She clearly is resistant to change."

If you want to look at the term within the context of Spitz's original observations, you could very easily conclude that the infants he and his colleagues observed in the foundling home were *not* suffering from an illness born of broken attachments, involuntary separation, and abandonment. Rather, like Joan, they were resisting change. Looked at in that way, the value of using resistance to change to explain the behavior of Noer's adults who had been subjected to reengineering and downsizing is no better than it is for explaining the behavior of Spitz's infants.

In fact, I would like to eliminate the concept of resistance to change from the vocabulary of organization life, because it does not accurately describe the phenomenon it purports to depict. From my point of view, what we call resistance to change is resistance to going through an experience of separation and alienation that probably will lead to the anaclitic depression blues. Assuming I am correct, an enlightened manager should say, "Joan is fighting my reengineered organizational structure that is going to make her lose her job, many of her friends, and contact with an organization that provides her with much of her sense of identity. Ultimately, she is resistant to suffering from the anaclitic depression blues that may make her sick and might even kill her. Given that, what can I do in my managerial leadership role that will mute or eliminate her fear of suffering the anaclitic depression blues?"

I have not received overwhelming support for my proposal to abandon the concept of resistance to change. Many of my fellow behavioral scientists (or behavioral artists, take your pick) are apparently resistant to suffering from the anaclitic depression blues that may strike them if they abandon a comfortable and popular but dysfunctional concept that in its hoary imprecision continues to provide us with a lot of emotional support—one part of which is financial in nature. After all, what would we lean on or call on for our emotional (and economic) support if we could not conduct seminars, write books, produce scholarly articles, and do consulting on the puzzling problem of overcoming resistance to change?

One possibility that comes to mind is that we could do training programs on the way in which Joan's resistance stems from an "invisible miasm . . . of an atmospheric-cosmic-telluric nature."

Regardless of how you answer that question, I am convinced that whatever level of misery exists in our organizations, the anaclitic depression blues frequently contributes to it. Furthermore, after thoroughly scouring the literature and observing everyday life, I have ascertained that the anaclitic depression blues *never* contributes to positive life experiences. That conclusion is particularly relevant to the practice of organizational leadership.

Anaclitic Depression and Leadership

In the opening pages of this chapter, I cited the work of Jaques and Clement (1991, p. 4), defining leadership as "that process in which one person sets the purpose or direction for one or more other persons and gets them to move along together with him or her and with each other in that direction with competence and full commitment." I also said that being a leader, according to that definition, requires that you be emotionally bonded, attached, connected, or linked with those whom you lead. It also requires that followers be similarly bonded, attached, connected, or linked with one another. In the absence of such bonds, you can coerce others into complying with your desires, but you can't lead them.

Accepting both the definition and the accompanying caveats, I have concluded that *when individuals in leadership roles take actions that create the anaclitic depression blues in themselves, in potential followers, or both, they weaken or eliminate the emotional linkages that are required for them to be effective leaders. At best, their capacity to lead is compromised; at worst, it is destroyed.*

For me, that is not an inconsequential thought. I don't know what it may be to you.

That Is the Football

The anaclitic depression blues is the football that is at the center of much of the work presented in this book. Following the rich tradition of Coach Lombardi, I have attempted to describe how I believe it relates to organizational behavior and the practice of leadership, as well as to life in general. In the following chapter, I kick around some of those ideas in greater detail. Specifically, I explore the manner in which our awareness of the anaclitic depression blues has the potential to assist each of us to function more effectively in our leadership roles.

That is the football.

I just hope you don't feel the need to join ranks with Max McGee by asking me to go over it all again.

How Come Every Time I Get Stabbed in the Back My Fingerprints Are on the Knife?

CHAPTER SEVEN

What If I Really Believe This Stuff?

After completing "Leadership and the Anaclitic Depression Blues," I lapsed into a reverie and asked myself, What if I actually believed this stuff? What if I really believe that leaders weaken or destroy their capacity to lead if their actions create the anaclitic depression blues in themselves and others? What difference, if any, would that belief make to me, Jerry B. Harvey, in my role as an organizational leader? Simultaneously, I mused about whether some of my leadership efforts in an academic institution might be relevant to others as they explore the process of leadership in environments where the halls are not enmeshed in ivy.

To address those questions, in this chapter I describe two fundamental approaches I have employed in an effort to apply my knowledge of leadership and the anaclitic depression blues to my role as a professorial leader. As I do so, I play around with the potential applicability of that knowledge to the manner in which others carry out their leadership roles.

Play with me, if you will.

Applying My Knowledge of Leadership and the Anaclitic Depression Blues to My Role as a Professor

I am a professor—a university professor, to be exact. Not everyone is impressed. My father-in-law, for instance, consistently introduced me to his domino-playing cronies as a carpenter even though I don't know one end of a hammer from another. When I asked him why he did it, he replied, "If they knew you made your living from just talking it would detract from our family's dignity, and I'm not about to embarrass my daughter in public."

Despite his biases, I remain a professor. In my role, I have a rich opportunity to engage in professorial leadership with students, nearly all of whom are at the graduate level. With them, I have attempted two generic approaches to deal with my hypothesized relationship between leadership and the anaclitic depression blues. First, I have redefined the meaning of cheating. Second, I have reduced the expression of objectivity in the classroom. See what you think and feel about each. More important, please

How Come Every Time I Get Stabbed in the Back My Fingerprints Are on the Knife?

think about whether these approaches might be relevant to the process of exercising leadership in other organizations, yours in particular.

Redefining Cheating

As you keep my professorial role in mind, I invite you to reminisce about your student days, including your experiences in the first grade and extending though your postgraduate studies, if any. Then answer the following question: During formal examinations, if a teacher catches students helping one another, what do we generally call the students' behavior? Most who have participated in any formal educational program will say, "cheating." In fact, virtually all formal educational institutions, particularly those known for their honor codes, say that giving and receiving aid on examinations is an unequivocal example of nefarious dishonesty, called cheating.

Do you find it peculiar that most of us in educational leadership roles believe that it is immoral for students to help one another during a time of need? Alternatively, do you find it puzzling that educational leaders, as a matter of institutional policy, require that their students be unhelpful, self-centered, narcissistic, and selfish, and then assert, with absolutely straight faces, that such behavior is a badge of honor? As I said in "Encouraging Future Managers to Cheat" (Harvey, 1988c), I believe such non*reasoning is bizarre, to say the least. (You will remember that non*reasoning is an active, energy-consuming process that one must engage in so as to keep from behaving rationally.) In fact, I am convinced that it is extremely destructive for people in leadership roles to teach members of any organization, academic or otherwise, that helping their colleagues is an immoral act. When organizational leaders require that potential followers be psychologically isolated from one another, they create an environment that frequently generates the anaclitic depression blues, with all of its destructive consequences.

Consequently, as a professorial leader who is interested in enhancing the performance of my educational organization (which includes me) by reducing or eliminating the anaclitic depression blues, I write the students in my introductory class a letter. I have found that I have to present my thoughts in writing so that students can assimilate the content at their convenience; they simply can't seem to understand what I say if I profess my point of view orally.

My letter reads as follows: "You may take examinations alone, with another person, or with as many other people as you like. 'Other people' includes classmates, parents, children, spouses, students from other classes, professors or 'hired guns.' I go absolutely blind with rage if I catch anyone cheating. *I define cheating as the failure to assist others on the exams if they request it*" (Harvey, 1997a).

How do you think our dean reacted when one of my outraged (and terrified) colleagues, apparently in an effort to avoid suffering from the anaclitic depression blues, showed him the letter? For starters, he invited me to his office for "a little discussion." The prospect of meeting with him dredged up long-repressed memories of the time Mrs. Sanders shipped me to Principal Beazley's office for dipping Mary Ann Gormley's blond pigtails in the inkwell of my desk.

The similarity of the experience was magnified when our dean, in a manner reminiscent of Mr. Beazley, began our discussion by threatening me with a severe case of anaclitic depression. Before he could fully activate my inborn fears of separation, rejection, and abandonment that frequently lead to full-blown cases of the anaclitic depression blues, he made a statement that caused me to break into prophylactic laughter. I want you to know that I wasn't laughing at him. Lord knows, all of us, the dean included, have enough misery in our respective lives without having others add to it by laughing at us rather than with us. I was laughing at the absurdity of the way in which we needlessly create bizarre, soul-shattering, anaclitically depressed organizational worlds for one another to live in, worlds that prevent us from fulfilling our God-given potentials, whatever those potentials may be.

He burst forth in a voice powerful enough to dislodge the green eyeshades from the furrowed brows of my beloved colleagues ensconced in the deep recesses of the accounting department, "Professor Harvey, are you aware of the absolute chaos that would be generated at The George Washington University if everyone began to help one another?"

Are you aware of the absolute chaos that would be generated at The George Washington University *if everyone began to help one another?*

What an extraordinarily relevant question for someone in a leadership role to ask—not only about The George

Washington University but also about any other organization. To his everlasting credit, though, the dean immediately followed up his pithy query with another that was equally, if not more, poignant in nature.

"Professor Harvey, did I just say what I think I said?" he asked.

"I'm pretty sure you did," I replied.

"Professor Harvey," he murmured quietly, "I believe I need to think about this issue some more on my own. Thanks for dropping by. I'm afraid that I may have learned more about myself and our school than I ever wanted to know. Perhaps we should continue our conversation at another time. I may give you another call, if you don't mind."

I suspect that the dean was afraid. No, I know he was afraid. Being separated from an idea that long has provided comfort and security frequently generates the anaclitic depression blues, and that is something about which it is legitimate to be afraid. It can make you sick. It can kill you.

Once I had redefined cheating within my own soul, and once the dean began to struggle with whether to redefine it in his, I began to think about other generic approaches I could take to apply my belief that one's capacity to lead is compromised or destroyed by taking actions that generate the anaclitic depression blues. That led to my exploration of the role of objectivity in the classroom and other organizations.

144

Reconsidering the Role of Objectivity

While reading *The Illusion of Technique,* in which William Barrett (1979) discusses the destructive impact of objectivity in human affairs, I began to explore the possibility that treating one another objectively in any organizational setting creates the anaclitic depression blues.

I commenced my exploration by constructing a Phrog Index, based on an article I wrote several years ago titled "Organizations as Phrog Farms" (Harvey, 1988b; Harvey, 1988c). The theme of the article is that an unstated purpose of many contemporary organizations is to turn good people into phrogs who lack the ability to think rationally, behave with courage, and respond to one another with honesty and compassion. Phrog is spelled with a *ph* because phrogs don't like to be known as phrogs and try to hide their phroginess in ways that are quite transparent to humans. The article includes brief discussions about the lonely life on the lily pad, the language of "ribbit," how bullphrogs get to be "fresident" and why cowphrogs seldom do. It also warns of the dangers inherent in kissing bullphrogs in the fog because, when you are surrounded by swamp fog, it is very difficult to ascertain the direction in which a bullphrog is facing.

The Phrog Index is designed to help us measure the degree to which we have adopted the ways of the swamp. Ultimately, it allows us to ascertain the amount of webbing between our respective toes. Constructed as a simple true-false test, the Index has one pair of items that stems from

Barrett's contention, based on Cartesian philosophy, that treating one another objectively creates loneliness and alienation, which, as you know, frequently causes the anaclitic depression blues.

The first item relevant to our discussion reads as follows: "It is very important that a manager be objective when dealing with subordinates on matters such as performance appraisal, pay, promotion and recognition." How do you think that most individuals in managerial leadership roles respond to that question? In my experience, approximately 90 percent reply, "true."

The next item in the Index reads, "I work most effectively with those who treat me as an object." How do most managers, virtually all of whom are held accountable for their work by a manager above them, answer that? As you might expect, nearly all say, "false." Why?

Well, as Barrett (1979) points out, when we treat others objectively we must *separate* ourselves from them and respond to them as objects in order to maintain our mastery over them. To be sure, we generally do it with the most honorable intentions, rationalizing that detaching ourselves from others and treating them as objects allows us to render fair and unbiased judgments about them. If we treat them as objects, however, how will they treat us in return? In my experience, they generally reciprocate and treat us as objects, too. So if you want to create widespread anaclitic depression in any organization, treat one another objectively—as objects that are inanimate, detached, separated, and alienated.

Being clear about the relationship of objectivity to anaclitic depression, I have maintained essentially the same definitions of cheating but have expanded my letter to the students in one of my advanced courses for which the topic of objectivity is integral to the course's conceptual content. The letter, in part, reads as follows:

> If you choose to enter the bureaucracy of this class and thereby receive a grade, you must submit a project, constituting a final examination, in which you communicate your understanding of the literature and experiences of the course.[1] The purposes of the project are: (a) to give you an opportunity to use the theory and research in ways that interest you or to be used by the theory in ways that don't, and (b) to give you an opportunity to express your competencies and incompetencies in a variety of ways. . . .
>
> Whatever you produce as a project must be presented in public. For example, if you write a paper, you must distribute it to all members of the class. If you sing and dance your creation titled "Bion's Basic Assumption Mental State Blues," you must sing and dance it for the total class. If you cook several theories of change, you must give us the opportunity to eat and, I hope, digest them.
>
> My reactions to your work will not be objective. They will be extremely subjective, subject to my competencies and incompetencies, all of which will be colored by my unique peculiarities and biases. Consequently, the major protection you have against any bureaucratic unfairness on my part is that anything I say to you about your work will be said in a format that you can share with others if you choose to do so, so that they can come to your aid if they choose to do so. [Harvey, 1997b]

Outcomes

As you can ascertain, I have attempted both to redefine cheating and to eliminate objectivity in an effort to mute or eliminate the anaclitic depression blues in my particular organization, the academic classroom. What has been the impact of my efforts? Here are some of the major outcomes, as I see them. In general, they relate to the incidence of cheating, curves of individual performance, and the quality—or character—of the work that is produced. By the way, I am going to discuss the outcomes of the separate courses as if I were discussing a single course. I do so because, for all intents and purposes, the outcomes of creating an organizational environment that reduces anaclitic depression have been the same.

Incidence of Cheating

In the twenty years since I implemented the policy that cheating is defined as the failure to assist others on exams if they request it, I am not aware of a single case of cheating by my students. That doesn't mean that cheating hasn't occurred. All I know is that no one has ever complained that others have cheated. I know for sure, though, that approximately 95 percent of those who have been associated with the class, including me, have opted to ask for assistance, to give assistance, or to do both during examinations. A small percentage have neither asked for assistance nor given it; but to my knowledge, no one who has asked for help has ever had someone refuse to provide it.

As far as I'm concerned, our desire to help and to be helped, to give aid and to receive it, and to be connected with others rather than alienated from them indicates that we have a massive reservoir of untapped human potential in academic organizations and other organizations as well. To tap that unused potential, those of us in leadership roles have to create organizational policies and structures that not only allow but also encourage everyone in the organization to provide one another with the technical aid and emotional support that each person needs in order to succeed.

If you are in an organizational leadership role and want to build a well-functioning team, you and your subordinates don't need to get your navels reamed out in team-building sessions, ropes courses, personality assessment seminars, or other contemporary forms of organizational dynamics programs (virtually all of which are conducted by a consultant who has no ongoing managerial accountability in your organization). As I said before, you need only to develop organizational policies and structures that mute, or eliminate, the anaclitic depression blues and thereby encourage all organizational members, yourself included, to behave normally.

Performance Curves

Once I attempted to reduce the threat of the anaclitic depression blues in my academic organization, I discovered that I virtually never obtain what are called normal or bell-shaped distributions of individual performance, an example of which is shown in Figure 7.1.

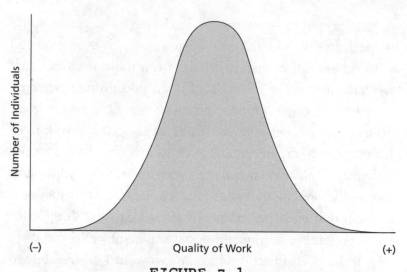

FIGURE 7.1.
"Normal" Performance of Anaclitically Depressed Population.

That should not come as a surprise, if you think about it. An underlying mathematical assumption of a bell-shaped curve is independence of the data, meaning that the probability of the occurrence of one event described in the curve is independent of, or unconnected with, the occurrence of any other event described in the same curve (Young and Veldman, 1972). For instance, the outcome of flipping one inanimate coin is not connected to the outcome of flipping another. To the best of our knowledge, one coin doesn't give a "flip" about what another coin does. Coins don't get angry, delighted, jealous, energized, lustful, nauseated, or greedy because other coins turn up heads or tails. The same cannot be said for the manner in which human beings toil together in work organizations.

The performances of individuals in organizations are, by their nature, interdependent. What one person does is connected with and affected by what others do. Peter Vaill's explanation that Ted Williams, the famous baseball player, was a .350 hitter only in context is an apt description of such interdependence (1978). What Vaill means is that one major reason for Mr. Williams's outstanding performance was that he consistently had excellent hitters who preceded and followed him in the batting order, thus making it very difficult for pitchers to concentrate their efforts solely on Williams. His performance was not independent of theirs nor were their performances independent of his.

For the same reason that Mr. Williams's performance was not independent of the performances of his teammates, the mathematical assumption of independence that underlies bell-shaped curves is not fulfilled when it comes to judging individual performances in work organizations, unless the members of the organization are forced by either the leader or organizational policy to be independent of one another. In that case, their state of enforced, alienated independence frequently causes them (including those in leadership roles) to suffer from the ravages of the anaclitic depression blues.

In the early classroom organizations in which I made a concerted effort to mute or eliminate the lonely independence that frequently results in the anaclitic depression blues, performance distributions were never bell shaped. Individual performances, *including my performance as the organization's leader,* consistently were skewed in the direction of high competence, as shown in Figure 7.2. As you

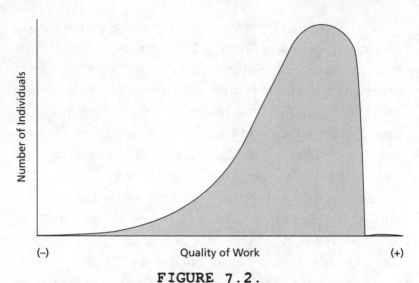

FIGURE 7.2.

Apparent Performance of Non-Anaclitically Depressed Population.

can see, most individuals appeared to perform very competently, a few did mediocre work, and almost no one produced work that was incompetent.

I didn't say "appeared to" without reason. Because I permitted students not only to assist one another but also to take their exams as groups, with everyone in the group receiving the same grade, I was unable to ascertain whether each of the individuals at the high end of the performance distribution *actually* performed competently. It is possible that some—or many—who appeared to be high performers might have performed incompetently but masked their incompetence by relying on the assistance they received from highly competent noncheaters.

As evidence of that possibility, I nearly always received a few complaints from individuals who said that "Sally didn't contribute anything to the examination, and that hacked us off" or that "Bill was totally unprepared for the exam, and I had to cover for him or else run the risk of being labeled by you as a cheater. It's not fair that he received an A in the examination when I was the one who really did the work."

Assuming the validity of those complaints (and I have no reason to doubt them), the *actual* distribution of individual performances was not nearly so skewed toward the high end of the performance scale as the grades would seem to indicate. Rather, most individuals probably were performing competently, but those about whom I received complaints actually were doing incompetent and, in some cases, exceedingly incompetent work. They were camouflaging their incompetence, though, by relying on the noncheaters to take care of them.

To explore that possibility, I attempted to follow Edward Deming's dictum that driving out fear is a fundamental requirement for organizational success. According to one of his famous Fourteen Points, an action required to accomplish that lofty goal is to eliminate formal performance appraisals entirely (Walton, 1986). I therefore attempted to eliminate the fear of anaclitic depression that is inherent in the process of formal performance appraisal, academic or otherwise. I tried to do that in a manner that also allowed the performance of each individual—good, bad, or indifferent—to be clearly visible to all members of the organization. That way, each of us would be "forced" to be more

153

aware of one another, and the students would not have individual, one-to-one, relationships with me when it came to displaying and evaluating their work or lack thereof.

As the professorial leader for still another course titled "Ethical, Moral, and Spiritual Issues of Organization," I changed the rules (that is, policies) governing the class so as to facilitate the kind of emotional attachment required to reduce or eliminate threats of anaclitic depression. Here are those rules, in truncated form:

> If you are willing to: (a) produce a brief essay each week about a moral, ethical or spiritual issue of organization that concerns you; (b) share your essay with everyone in the class; (c) discuss your essay with others during class time, and (d) write a critique of each person's essay and return it to him or her by the following class period, you will receive an A in the course. There is no other grade.
>
> I will produce an essay each week under the same conditions, except I won't receive a formal grade. If you are unwilling to work within the framework of those rules or are uninterested in doing so, please do not take the course. [Harvey, 1997c]

Within those parameters, I find that the curves of actual individual performance (meaning the actual quality of work that the students produce as individuals, without reference to the grades they receive) are consistently bimodal. That distribution is described in Figure 7.3. As I suspected would be the case, when the threat of anaclitic depression is reduced to a minimum, a higher percentage of individuals performs incompetently than you get in a bell-shaped distribution; almost nobody does mediocre work; and the

How Come Every Time I Get Stabbed in the Back My Fingerprints Are on the Knife?

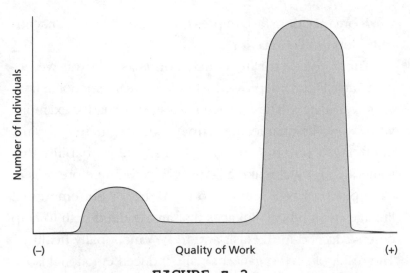

FIGURE 7.3.

Actual Performance of Non–Anaclitically Depressed Population.

overwhelming majority of participants (myself included) performs work that is highly competent.

These findings are derived from observations of approximately fifteen ten-person academic organizations for which I have served as the professorial leader. In my role, I clearly have not been independent of those whose performances I judged, and, by design, the students are not independent of me or of one another. Therefore, my observations are essentially clinical in nature and for that and other reasons certainly do not meet the rigorous standards of the scientific method. Nevertheless, the consistency with which I, and a few colleagues who have tried the same approach, have observed these phenomena has led me to hypothesize that bell-shaped distributions of performance in *work* organizations are expressions of abnormal, anaclitically depressed behavior.

The rationale for my conclusion is as follows. We become anaclitically depressed when we break emotional linkages with others. These broken linkages occur, for example, when a professorial leader "curves" grades, thereby saying, in effect, "If one person makes an A, the probability that someone else will make an A is reduced. Therefore, it is in each person's best interest to break his or her emotional linkages with others, linkages that are required both to help others succeed in the task and to be emotionally healthy." The result of such organizationally induced emotional isolation is, frequently, the expression of psychological and spiritual alienation known as the anaclitic depression blues. (For further discussion, see Chapter Six.)

Applying Knowledge of the Anaclitic Depression Blues Outside the Academic Environment

Looking outside the academic environment, I am convinced that we can easily apply the same argument to the rather common organizational policy of basing formal performance appraisals or compensation schemes on the underlying assumption that the distribution of human performance in work organizations is inevitably bell shaped. If you, in a

156

How Come Every Time I Get Stabbed in the Back My Fingerprints Are on the Knife?

managerial leadership role, place your faith in and worship at the altar of the First Church of the Universal Bell-Shaped Curve, you must give a very limited percentage of "outstanding" ratings and a very limited percentage of "poor" ratings to your subordinates. All other members of your organization, then, must fall into various predetermined gradations in the middle of the curve. Once you make the decision to accept the sanctity of that dogma, all organizational members are encouraged to be concerned about themselves and not about others, because helping others succeed reduces one's own possibility of receiving a high performance rating and the promotions or increases in compensation that frequently accompany it. Such forced isolation frequently culminates, once again, in the anaclitic depression blues.

Given the nature of my observations, I have a suggestion that you might want to pursue in your organizational leadership role to test my hypothesis that, in work organizations, a bimodal distribution is "normal" when the threat of anaclitic depression is muted or eliminated. First, take whatever steps you can to reduce the anaclitic depression blues in your organization. Then rate the performances of all individuals for whom you are directly accountable. Rate their performances not within the framework of the forced bell-shaped curve required by the High Priests of Human Resource Management but as you *actually* experience the quality of their work. For example, if you are accountable for the work of twenty subordinates and believe that eighteen have performed in an outstanding manner and two have done work that is incompetent, rate them in that way.

If you believe that all twenty have performed gloriously, rate them that way. If you believe that all of them have been "duds," rate them that way. Forget about distributing your ratings according to the ostensibly "immutable" laws of the bell-shaped curve that forces them into a predetermined pattern.

When I have asked individuals in managerial leadership roles to carry out this exercise, I have found that they frequently report something like this: "Well, I have ten people who report to me. Nine are real solid contributors, and one is a monumental screw-up. And you know, a funny thing happens every time the screw-up leaves the organization. Just as I am about to let out with a sigh of relief, one of the people who has been doing well suddenly falls apart and takes the screw-up's place. Even crazier, a lot of times when we have an opportunity to recruit someone to take the place of our 'disaster,' we go out and hire someone who turns out to be as bad or worse. It seems as if we have to have at least one lousy performer fouling things up or we aren't happy."

The frequency with which I have seen the bimodal curve of performance in organizations has led me to hypothesize the following: given two organizations in which the work skills of the individual members are equal, the performances of individuals in the anaclitically depressed organization will be distributed "normally," congruent with the parameters of the bell-shaped curve. However, in the organization in which the anaclitic depression blues is either muted or eliminated, the performances of individual members will be bimodal, with most people doing outstanding work, very few people doing work that is mediocre, and noticeably more than you get in a bell-shaped curve doing work that is downright incompetent. Furthermore, I have become convinced that virtually all high-performing organizations have that form of bimodal performance distribution.

Although organizational leaders may strive for "zero-defects" organizations in which each member performs at the high end of the competency scale, I never have seen an organization of any sort that is able to maintain that type of distribution over an extended period of time. Even God failed to accomplish that lofty goal with a motley little organization of apple pickers in the Garden of Eden, and I haven't seen anyone else succeed at the task. Have you?

And why haven't they been successful?

The Contributions of Low Performers in High-Performing Organizations

Well, I have concluded that high-performing organizations *need* the low performers; those people help the organization *as a whole* perform well, regardless of the organization's task. The low performers fulfill several very important organizational functions.

Benchmarks

Low performers provide needed benchmarks for assessing competence. Without the low performers serving as a basis for comparison, the other members of the organization don't know when they are doing well. Fish are the last to know they are in water.

Sources of Turmoil

Low performers provide a constant source of anxiety, tension, and uproar that serves to energize the organization as a whole. That's not a new thought. It has been around since 1951, when Stanley Schacter demonstrated that the presence of a disruptive, incompetent deviant in an otherwise competent decision-making group enhances the quality of the work by the total group (1951). Low performers have such an effect even though the competent members of the group want to get rid of the low performers because of their disruptiveness. Like Schacter, I have never found a bimodally distributed, high-performing organization whose members are comfortable with having the low performers around. I have found a few organizations whose members are perceptive and disciplined enough to recognize that the low (or otherwise disruptive) performers are important contributors to their organization's high performance and that getting rid of the low performers serves only to bite a hand that feeds the organization as a whole. In that case, the high performers learn to tolerate the low performers, sometimes with grace, but that's about all.

When organizational members lack that combination of disciplined perceptivity and tolerance, they frequently convince the managerial leader to fire the low performers. Once the low performers are fired, however, a significant number of the high performers, contrary to all conventional logic, frequently develop the anaclitic depression blues that is characteristic of Layoff Survivor's Syndrome, and their performances drop. In addition, for reasons that I have not yet figured out, some of those comprised in the "bump" at

How Come Every Time I Get Stabbed in the Back My Fingerprints Are on the Knife?

the low end of the bimodal curve improve their performances. The result is a bell-shaped curve of mediocre organizational performance, as seen in Figure 7.4.

Japanese organizations are examples of work organizations that have learned to tolerate individual incompetence in the service of organizational excellence. My colleagues in the international organizational consulting business tell me that Japanese organizations are known for their complements of incompetent "window people." Those individuals actually sit at the physical periphery of the organization, near the windows, doing work that is basically useless but that at the same time won't hurt anyone or get the organization as a whole in trouble.

Outside the realm of formal work organizations, most healthy, high-performing extended families have a hell-raising troublemaker whose role is to help the family as a whole function well. If you don't believe that, think about it during your annual family reunion, when Aunt Nell gets tipsy for the twenty-third consecutive time, insults gentle Uncle Fred, and then concludes her contribution to the family's overall well-being by puking in the soup. Everybody in the family faithfully complains about her. In clandestine backyard meetings, they agree not to invite her to next year's dinner. Yet when invitations are sent out for the following reunion, the family capitulates and invites her "one more time." They do so because they need her. In fact, they can't imagine not having her there.

Should you want to get theological about the matter in the domain of individual behavior, the bump at the low end of the bimodal distribution can be considered to be a

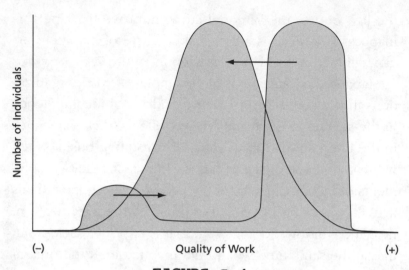

FIGURE 7.4.
Performance Change When High-Performing Population
Becomes Anaclitically Depressed.

metaphorical expression of the doctrine of original sin, a
Christian theological belief system that says each of us, no
matter how compulsively we strive for moral perfection, is
inherently flawed (Brandon, 1970). According to some theologians who have that point of view, Adam and Eve were
the first examples of the doctrine in action, and the hun-
dreds of generations that have followed them have not
been able to improve on their inherent imperfection. If
Charles Darwin's thesis of survival of the fittest is correct,
such imperfection, found both in individuals and organizations, must serve a positive role in the survival of the
species; otherwise, the imperfection would disappear.

Outlets for Altruism

Finally, the individuals who constitute the bump at the low end of the bimodal distribution provide a needed outlet for the expression of altruism. George Vaillant defines altruism as "constructive and instinctively gratifying service to others," the process of "getting pleasure from giving to others what you yourself would like to receive" (1974, p. 110). According to Vaillant, all of us need to give to others if we are to maintain a sense of well-being; and, because of that need, altruism is one of the most constructive expressions of mental health. Those of us who work with individuals in leadership roles who stress the importance of having "lean and mean" organizations know that a dash of altruism provides a welcome relief from the anaclitic depression blues that leanness and meanness generate in everyone other than sadists and masochists. Such relief applies to those who practice altruism as well as to those who benefit from it.

The Composition of the Bump

Who are these individuals who compose the bump at the low end of the bimodal distribution that is characteristic of non–anaclitically depressed, high-performing organizations?

As best I can ascertain, they fall into two subgroups. The first consists of individuals who, in the terms of Elliott Jaques and Kathryn Cason (1994), lack the inborn capability to do the work. No amount of training, education, coaching, or energizing by the leader or others will get them to the point where they can do the tasks they have been assigned. They simply are not up to doing the work, period.

The second group is composed of individuals who have made poor choices about how to go about doing their work or who have confronted a set of circumstances that temporarily prevents them from working at their levels of potential capability. Virtually all of us have had that experience. The quality of our work has suffered when we have pursued poorly conceived plans, struggled with health problems, been absorbed by family troubles, sunk into the despair of midlife crisis, or grappled with learning an unfamiliar technology. But our temporary descent into the world of incompetence has been short lived, and before long we have worked ourselves back into the group at the top of the heap.

Considering the composition of the bump, I have come to understand that at any given moment, approximately 5 to 10 percent of the individuals in high-performing organizations must be incompetent to perform their work. Knowing that, I am thinking about starting an employment agency that will provide you with incompetent people in whatever area of inexpertness you need them in order to help you, in your leadership role, raise your organization's overall performance. Preliminary market testing of the idea leads me to believe that it may be an idea whose time has not yet come—but I believe it will.

Reactions to My Attempts to Eliminate the Anaclitic Depression Blues in the Classroom

How do you think students react when they get the letter that redefines cheating and describes my approach to the problem of eliminating organizational objectivity? For starters, several generally drop the course. In a recent class, seven out of thirty headed for the door. As they disappeared into the flickering neon lights of the hallway, one turned and with venom in his voice said, "I took this class to learn how to be a manager. I don't want to waste my time worrying about anyone other than myself."

From those who remain, I receive all sorts of intriguing questions. Some ask, "Do you really mean what you say?" Others ask if I have been drinking. One asked if I had been hit on the head with a brick on the way to class. I think my all-time favorite came from a doctoral student for whom this was his last course. During the discussion about examinations, he inquired in a tremulous voice that betrayed a sense of growing fear and desperation, "Specifically, what do you want me to do?"

"Do something that interests you," I replied.

"What interests me?" he asked, oblivious to the poignancy of his question.

Here was a doctoral student, on the verge of receiving a Ph.D. degree, who had no interests. What a tragedy. What a perfect example of someone who had been in an ana-clitically depressed academic environment for so long that he had lost his capacity to think. Had the student been a professional football player, even Coach Lombardi might have had difficulty providing him with an environment in which he could learn the essence of the game. Regardless of how Coach Lombardi might have coped with the doctoral student, one of you may have hired him.

Nevertheless, in an environment where I have made an effort to reduce or eliminate the anaclitic depression blues, the great majority of students consistently have performed work of a qualitatively different nature than the work produced by students suffering from the blues.

For instance, Dorothy (a pseudonym), whose hobby was gourmet cooking, enlisted the assistance of several classmates and cooked five theories of management. The other members of the class attended a formal dinner at her house and ate them. Four days later, the chair of a faculty committee that governed Dorothy's academic program asked where he could find Dorothy's examination. I informed him what, to the best of my knowledge, was the exact location.

David, a naval officer who had commanded a missile cruiser the previous year, sang his examination to the tune of "The HMS Pinafore." Accompanied by his son, an accomplished pianist, David performed his examination in full-dress ceremonial naval regalia, including an antique three-cornered hat and a golden sword swinging at his side. He had a terrible voice, but his lyrics were rigorous expressions of the major theoretical concepts of the course.

Terry announced that he was going to juggle concepts from Wilfred Bion's very difficult book, *Experiences in Groups* (1961). I, and others, thought he meant that he was going to juggle the concepts intellectually. It turned out, though, that Terry is a semiprofessional juggler who had occasionally performed in circuses. He brought a tape deck, turned on music, pulled three balls from his back pocket, and juggled for approximately half an hour. When he completed his juggling routine, everyone knew the essence of Bion's work. If my memory serves correctly, Terry subsequently collected several consulting fees for juggling Bion's theory at professional meetings that focused on group dynamics.

Thirteen students worked together to write, advertise, produce, and perform their examination as a play titled *Alice in OD Land*. Maintaining the basic literary integrity of Lewis Carroll's classic while performing it in full costume (including a six-foot-four-inch, 260-pound White Rabbit) in the drama department's theater, the group expressed the realities, absurdities, and illusions of the organizational development movement. The event drew approximately 175 people, each of whom paid $2 apiece to see the production. After their performance, one of my colleagues wrote the dean of the school and demanded that I be disciplined or fired because my students were engaging in frivolous activities unrelated to the practice of management. Responding to my colleague's missive, the dean (this time) squelched my fear of suffering from the anaclitic depression blues with a terse one-line reply, copying it to me. He said, "Dear Professor Williams: Any time 175 people are

167

willing to pay $2 apiece to see an examination you give, let me know and I will be at that one, too."

One of my all-time favorite exams, though, and one from which I learned an enormous amount, was done by Betsy. Although she did it approximately twenty years ago (as you can tell by the organizational theories that were in vogue at the time), I feel as if it occurred only yesterday.

Unbeknownst to us, Betsy had been a professional singer and dancer, but at the time of her examination, she was pursuing an M.B.A. degree. As permitted by the rules of the exam, Betsy brought a male professional singer and dancer to perform with her. He was dressed as a vaudeville usher. As we entered the dance studio where she presented her exam, he was holding a placard that read, "Betsy Monroe Presents the Management Theory Review." At the appointed hour, music from *Hello, Dolly* wafted across the stage, and she and her partner began to sing and dance Douglas McGregor's classic managerial assumptions (1960) about the nature of humankind, Theories X and Y. "Hello Dougie, well, hello Dougie. It's so nice to have our values where they belong." With her partner in a supporting role, she performed Abraham Maslow's hierarchy of needs (1954) as an emerging flower. She became a marionette as they interpreted B. F. Skinner's work on behaviorism (1938). She summarized my work on the Abilene Paradox within the musical framework of "The Wedding March" from Wagner's *Lorengrin*. For the grand finale, she surrendered her partner as she sang and danced Jack Gibb's trust theory (Bradford, Gibb, and Benne, 1964), her interpretation of which was that individual and organizational growth occurs as a function of the *stripping* of defenses.

I believe that I can safely say that no one who was present will *ever* forget Gibb's theory or the way in which Betsy presented it. In fact, she received the only standing ovation I have ever seen for a final examination. Furthermore, her unexpected approach to communicating otherwise dry academic theory led me to understand that what most of us in organizational leadership roles worship as "individuality" is, in reality, the subjective experience of uniqueness that we receive in organizations *only when we are not threatened with the anaclitic depression blues.*

As I have said, not everyone finds individual success in a non–anaclitically depressed, high-performing organization. Charles, for example, produced an excruciating twenty-minute snare drum solo that communicated absolutely nothing about the concepts of the course. It required all the altruism we could muster to tolerate it. His inept presentation, which clearly fell into the incompetent bump of the bimodal distribution, was so disastrous that it was extremely difficult for us to discuss our perceptions of his work with him. To put it mildly, he clearly had made a lousy decision about how to communicate his knowledge of management theory to the other members of the organization.

If you, in your leadership role, try to eliminate or mute the anaclitic depression blues in your organization, would the qualitative character of individual performances change as dramatically as it has in mine? Even more to the point, would it change at all for the better? I believe it would. In fact, I would bet on it. But I can't say for sure. I know of only one way for you to answer that question to *your* satisfaction . . .

So What If I Do Really Believe This Stuff?

Betsy's performance, together with virtually all the others I have experienced in my professorial leadership role, has led me anew to the following conclusion. Effective leadership, the process by which we set the direction for others and get them to move along with us and one another in that direction with competence and commitment, occurs most often in organizations in which we don't threaten one another with the anaclitic depression blues. My experiences have strengthened my conviction that any interpersonal act, policy, or structure which creates anaclitic depression generally inhibits and sometimes completely destroys our ability to exercise organizational leadership. It doesn't destroy the possibility of exercising influence by coercion, however. Unfortunately, we sometimes incorrectly call coercion *leadership* rather than *despotism* and, in the process, create enormous misery for ourselves and others.

I have therefore concluded that one of the most powerful acts of leadership for any individual in a leadership role is to develop the interpersonal discipline or to design organizational processes, procedures, structures, and poli-

How Come Every Time I Get Stabbed in the Back My Fingerprints Are on the Knife?

cies that by their nature provide organization members with emotional support rather than threaten them with the anaclitic depression blues. I think my friend and colleague Elliott Jaques has come nearer than anyone I know to describing, in a systematic fashion, how to accomplish that lofty goal. Unfortunately, his work is not very well known. In fact, when his name is mentioned, most leaders, followers, consultants, and organizational theorists ask, "Who the hell is Elliott Jaques?" That is a great question to ask, and I hope to answer it in the subsequent chapter.

Amen.

CHAPTER EIGHT

Musing About the Elephant in the Parlor or "Who the Hell Is Elliott Jaques?"

S everal years ago, a respected colleague mentioned
that he had come across a very different book in the
field of management and organization, titled *A General
Theory of Bureaucracy* (1976), by someone named Elliott
Jaques.

"Who the hell is Elliott Jaques?" said I.

After providing a synopsis of the author's background
that he had obtained from the book jacket, my colleague
said, "Regardless of who he is, you ought to read it. He
thinks in peculiar ways—very much like you. He's just a
lot smarter; on a different stratum, one might say."

Acutely aware of my colleague's sarcasm but naive as
to his perceptive, precise understanding and application of
Jaques's concept of *stratum,* a major theoretical construct
of his Stratified Systems Theory (SST), I went to our library
and checked out the one copy of *A General Theory* that our
beloved institution owned. That action itself was instructive.
The book had rested—or, more accurately, slept—in the

stacks for nearly three years. During that period, my colleague and I were apparently the only members of the entire university community who had seen fit to check it out. "It's certainly not one of our most sought-after books dealing with management," said our friendly librarian.

Despite its absence from the *New York Times* best-seller list, I read it and found it to be one of the most creative, stimulating, exciting, rigorous, confrontational, intellectually demanding, and morally provocative pieces of work I had ever read in the field of management and organizational behavior. No, that's not accurate. I found it to be *the* most creative, stimulating, exciting, rigorous, confrontational, intellectually demanding, and morally provocative piece of work I had ever read in the field of management and organizational behavior.

In light of my reaction, I began to wonder how I, who pride myself as being a semibright, relatively well read professional in the field of organizational behavior, had not heard of Jaques's work. Despite the librarian's comment, I began to have the fearful thought that I was an anomaly; and I began to experience the pangs of separation anxiety we frequently suffer when we suddenly and inexplicably find ourselves alone in a crowd.

Fortunately, or unfortunately, depending on one's particular bias, I found that I was far from being sui generis. In fact, when I conducted an ongoing informal poll of academic colleagues, fellow consultants, clients, graduate students, managers, participants at corporate training seminars, human resource directors, and others who I believed would, or should, have reason to know something about Elliott

How Come Every Time I Get Stabbed in the Back My Fingerprints Are on the Knife?

Jaques and SST, I discovered that virtually none of those I interviewed had heard of him either.

Oh, I did find a couple of exceptions. One interviewee asked, "Isn't he the fellow who wrote a book about the problems involved in changing the cultures of factories?" (Jaques, 1951). Another said, "I think he's the psychiatrist who did an article a long time ago called 'Death and the Midlife Crisis' [Jaques, 1965]. If memory serves correctly, it had something to do with all the flack that hits you during middle age. If he's the guy I have in mind, that was an excellent piece of work. I have always wondered what happened to him. Since I've never seen anything else he's written, I assume he's dead."

On the whole, though, "Who the hell is Elliott Jaques?" or some variation thereof was a stock reply that echoed in the backroads of my inquiring mind. In fact, I heard the question with such monotonous frequency that I associated it with a story I had heard about an eccentric CEO of a megacorporation who housed a huge, powerful, stately elephant in the parlor of his New York penthouse. When guests visited the CEO, the elephant, in its grandiose, domineering manner, would meander to and fro about the room, brushing against them, the furniture, the walls, and the chandeliers. Nevertheless, for reasons known only to the CEO's Great Manager in the Sky, few of the visitors acknowledged its presence. In fact, when the host showed them to the door and said, "Incidentally, what did you think about the elephant in my parlor?" most replied quizzically, "What elephant?"

As you might surmise, I am impressed by the similarity between the guests' responses to the elephant and the reaction, by and large, that individuals who have an avowed interest in the theory and practice of management and organizational behavior have had to Jaques's work. That is, when confronted with the reality of a piece of seminal thinking, stately and sweeping in its design, scientifically testable, powerful in its capacity to deal with the world of which it is a part, massive in its implications for individuals and organizations of all kinds, and even more impressive when viewed in comparison with other works of pissant proportions that attempt to address some of the same issues, why do so many in the field of organizational behavior respond with "What's Stratified Systems Theory?" "Who the hell is Elliott Jaques?" or some other equivalent of "What elephant?" And that question takes on added significance when one realizes that since 1952 the elephant has produced numerous articles and eighteen books about SST starting with *The Changing Culture of a Factory* and including, most recently, his work in conjunction with Kathryn Cason, *Human Capability* (Jaques and Cason, 1994).

Consequently, in this chapter, I would like to muse a bit about the work of my friend and colleague Elliott Jaques, a metaphorical elephant who resides in organizational parlors throughout the world. More specifically, I would like to start by giving a summary of his theory in the context of what a moderately sophisticated knowledge of SST would potentially allow someone to accomplish. I take this approach because SST is a megatheory of organization, and I doubt that I, or anyone else for that matter, can do it justice in a simple summary. Once I have outlined what I believe to be SST's basic tenets and its potential applicability to life in organizations, I will focus on why I think a fecund work of such extraordinary creativity and importance has been virtually ignored by managers, consultants, and academicians.

As I go about my musing, please keep in mind that as I talk about Elliott Jaques personally and about his work on SST, I am speaking about them interchangeably. I say this because I agree with one of the basic assumptions of SST: that an isomorphic relationship inevitably exists between each of us individuals and the work we are capable of producing. More important, it assumes that given the particular mix of inborn capability combined with the knowledge, skills, values, and temperament we bring to a task, an isomorphic relationship exists between us and the work we *do* produce (Jaques and Cason, 1994).

What Knowledge of SST Potentially Allows You to Do

The following are some of what I believe to be SST's potential contributions to the field of management and organizational behavior.

1. SST provides guidelines for building a Requisite Organization, the design of which facilitates getting work done and, at the same time, generates feelings of trust and security among its members (Jaques, 1996). In my language, I would say that SST increases members' freedom to work by reducing the amount of energy they waste through suffering from the anaclitic depression blues.

2. SST provides you with a comprehensive, univocal language of organizational behavior. Jaques rigorously defines such terms as *work, task, bureaucracy, association, manager, level, leadership, knowledge, values,* and *skill.* Once you know the definitions, you will be able to carry on conversations about bureaucracy and other forms of organization with the same precision that physicists employ when they discuss ergs. If you don't think that the capacity to communicate in rigorous terms is a significant advance in the field of organizational behavior, ask twenty physicists to define *erg.* No matter what language they speak or what school they attended or what employment experiences they have had, each of them will define *erg* in the same way. Alternatively, ask twenty organizational development (OD) consultants, human resource development professionals, or line managers to define *bureaucracy, OD,* or *leader.* Although they generally curse bureaucracy, tout the virtues of OD, and worship good leaders, virtually no two of these people will produce identical definitions of the terms. In short, they don't know what each other is talking about. And if we don't know what we are talking about, carrying on a literate conversation about "it," whatever the "it" may be, becomes downright difficult, if not impossible.

3. If you are employed in a hierarchical organization, SST allows you to tell exactly how many levels your organization should have in order to facilitate work, reduce paranoia, increase trust, and minimize those anaclitic depression blues. For instance, SST shows you why even the largest and most complex hierarchical organizations in the world need only eight levels. If they have more than eight, they will be overmanaged: the antirequisite design of the organization, itself, will add needless financial and emotional overhead that comes from having too many people in managerial roles attempting to micromanage people who don't need or want to be managed and won't cooperate with anyone who tries to manage them. Using SST, you need know only one piece of information—the targeted completion time (measured in days, weeks, months, or years) of the longest single task on which your organization's CEO is working (Jaques and Cason, 1994). Once you have that information, which is called the Time Span of Discretion (TSD) of a work role, you will know how many levels your organization should have in order to be "requisite." You may not want such information to be widely shared, though, because once you and others possess it, many of the "political" factors that underlie your organization's design will be eliminated. Stated differently, it will become very difficult to justify "layering in" Fred as a vice president just because he is your brother-in-law.

4. SST allows you to ascertain, within very small limits, how much employees in any managerial accountability hierarchy will feel is a fair amount to be compensated for their work. All you have to know is the TSD of their particular work roles. The correlation between that single variable and what the person believes is fair compensation, termed *Felt-Fair Pay* (Jaques, 1976, p. 228) is .89 to .93 (Richardson, 1971). The longer our TSD, the more money—in dollars, pesos, pounds, and so on—we believe we should receive for our work. The shorter the TSD, the less money we believe we should get. You don't even need to know what the person's work role is, how much seniority the person has, what the person's educational level is, or whether the person is in a managerial, staff, or technical role. You can calculate the Felt-Fair Pay for large groups of people very rapidly without a lot of pomp and circumstance. I wonder why organizations involved in consultation about compensation schemes apparently are unfamiliar with such a simple, straightforward approach for solving what most of them contend is a very complex problem.

5. SST allows you to measure a person's potential for serving in an infinite variety of leadership roles, including managerial leadership, parental leadership, political leadership, military leadership, and so on, by knowing the length of time—measured in days, weeks, months, or years—that the person can work into the future without knowing the outcome of his or her work. Called *capability,* that potential is ultimately your capacity to cope with complexity as you work (Jaques and Cason, 1994). The greater your capability, the more complex are the prob-

How Come Every Time I Get Stabbed in the Back My Fingerprints Are on the Knife?

lems you can solve. The less your capability, the less complex are the problems you can solve. According to Jaques, a person's basic capability is inborn and matures along a predictable trajectory, from birth to death, and that trajectory cannot be altered by education, hard work, perseverance, or training. Once you know about capability, you will also know why the styles of leaders are irrelevant to getting work done, why personality is relevant to leaders' success only if they are psychotic or deeply neurotic, why you can't train individuals to think strategically, and why leaders must have greater capability than their followers in order to lead them.

6. SST shows you how to measure the leadership potential of anyone in a particular organizational role by talking with that person about a subject in which he or she is interested. In a startling finding, Jaques shows you how to predict, with high validity, who, at age twenty-five, will or will not have the capability to successfully carry out the role of being a competent president (or vice president, general manager, or first-line supervisor) of your organization twenty years later (Jaques and Cason, 1994). If you are interested in succession planning in your organization, such data might merit your close attention.

7. SST shows you the significant differences in organizational dynamics that are created by organizations structured as associations as opposed to those structured as accountability hierarchies. So you will know the basic difference, an association is a group of people who come together to pursue a common interest, develop some rules to govern themselves, and select one or more of their members to administer the rules on their behalf. An accountability hierarchy (generally called a bureaucracy), in contrast, is a stratified organization in which one person is accountable for the work of one or more others and enforces that accountability through the right to veto appointments, assign tasks, evaluate performance, and remove from role those individuals whose work is not satisfactory.

Once you become aware of these differences, you will know why sending people to ropes courses, sensitivity training, or team-building sessions is inherently counterproductive both for them and for their organizations, if they work in an accountability hierarchy, as do 90 percent of the people in the United States. You will also know why the practice of medicine, the generation and transmission of new ideas and knowledge, and the exploration of sacred beliefs are inevitably compromised by organizations structured as accountability hierarchies. Likewise, SST clarifies why the routine production of goods and services is most effectively carried out in organizations designed as accountability hierarchies, why it is destructive to the human psyche to try to get rid of hierarchy in any organization, and why movements designed to eliminate hierarchy are inherently absurd.

Have I overstated the potentials of SST? Probably. The only way for you to find out for sure, though, is to read one or more of the eighteen books Jaques has written.

How Come Every Time I Get Stabbed in the Back My Fingerprints Are on the Knife?

Have I overstated the potentials of SST any more dramatically than the missionaries for such managerial panaceas as empowerment, zero-based budgeting, sensitivity training, management by objectives, total quality management, learning organizations, the Myers-Briggs Type Indicator, organizational development, managerial style, or reengineering have overstated the potentials of their religions? Probably not. Yet virtually all professionals in the field of organizational behavior have read about, discussed, seen videos extolling, or gone to soul-saving seminars to become acquainted with one if not all of those messianic approaches to organizational resurrection. So I again raise the question, Why is SST not better known by professionals in the field, or, metaphorically speaking, Why have we for the most part ignored the elephant in our parlor?

To provide order to what otherwise could be chaos, I begin this discussion with several rationales for such ignore-ance *(sic)* that I have rejected and tell you why I have seen fit to do so. Then I suggest an explanation that I believe will, over time, turn out to be valid. Finally, I discuss what I believe is the major potential contribution of SST to the world of both formal and informal management and organization and perhaps to the world at large.

Rejected Explanations

Let's start with some proposed explanations I have rejected and the reasons underlying my rejections.

Jaques Doesn't Communicate His Ideas Very Well

Many individuals who have read one or more of Jaques's articles and books (particularly his earlier ones) or who have heard him speak in person about his work contend that some of their reservations regarding SST stem from the fact that Jaques is neither a poetic writer nor a charismatic speaker. Such criticism is frequently registered in concrete terms, such as, "If he wants his work to be understood, he ought to write a simple book like *The One-Minute Manager*," or "He doesn't speak with the evangelical zeal, the melodious rhythm, and the drumbeat cadence of a Tom Peters exhorting the masses to embrace organizational excellence."

I too am aware that much of Jaques's writing style doesn't have quite the literary quality of a Shakespearean sonnet (although it has improved significantly as he has worked with his foremost collaborator, Kathryn Cason). I also am aware that his talks about SST don't exactly conjure up such images as those evoked by Winston Churchill speaking to the British Empire about blood, sweat, and tears. Consequently, I have nearly been seduced at times into believing that his deserved influence has suffered, if not from his own communication deficiencies, then from a shortage of competent "translators."

Ultimately, though, I have concluded that such criticism of his work is irrelevant. It's irrelevant because, if one listens carefully both to supporters and detractors of SST who offer that argument, they frequently follow it up with such

How Come Every Time I Get Stabbed in the Back My Fingerprints Are on the Knife?

statements as "I had to read his damn book five times before I thought I understood it; but each time I reread it, I understood it better" or "After Jaques concluded his talk to our group, a half-dozen of us sat in my office and discussed what he had said for three hours." Because the very people who claim that Jaques lacks communication skills frequently reread and fervently debate what he supposedly hasn't communicated, I have decided that he must communicate something fairly well. Realizing that, I have also gained a renewed appreciation of the validity of a point Jaques made during a rambling discourse to participants in a faculty seminar on the topic of leadership at The George Washington University (Jaques, 1990a). Specifically, he said that the influence of leaders stems from the fact that "they have competence [meaning "capability"] to burn and, one way or another, they communicate that competence to others." I can only wonder what might happen if Jaques were to develop Shakespearean or Churchillian communication skills. Some fairly well known people in leadership roles have been crucified for considerably less; one can only guess what might happen to an elephant.

Jaques Contends That Basic Human Capability and Consequent Leadership Potential Is Inborn and Cannot Be Changed

Apparently, we are residents of a world in which it is politically correct to assert that, with hard work and perseverance, anyone can grow up to be president, compose like Wolfgang Amadeus Mozart, sing like Luciano Pavarotti, act like Jessica Tandy, think like Albert Einstein, write like Jean-Paul Sartre, or manage like Alfred Sloan. Therefore, when Jaques says that human capability is inborn, some people complain that he violates the democratic principles that our sexist forefather Thomas Jefferson set forth in the Declaration of Independence when he said, "All men are created equal." Yet those same people, if asked directly if they think they could sing like Pavarotti, will admit that they don't believe they could, no matter how much they practiced and how hard they tried. "I just wasn't born with the right stuff," they will say. Furthermore, if they see a six-foot-ten-inch, 265-pound young man with hands large enough to permit him to carry a basketball as though it were a Concord grape, they readily admit that genes have provided him with the potential for playing a game called basketball in a manner that they, at five-foot-one and 103 pounds, couldn't possibly emulate. In short, although we may raise Cain about Jaques's contention that leadership capability is essentially inborn, when the crunch comes, virtually everyone admits that much of our capability to carry out a wide variety of tasks in everyday life *is* inborn. Consequently, I don't pay much attention to that argument when it comes to ignoring Jaques's work.

SST Can Be Understood Only by Persons in the Upper Strata of Capability

According to Jaques, your capability—your capacity to deal with complexity as you go about solving problems—can be ascertained by measuring your time-horizon—the longest time span with which you can currently cope (Jaques and Cason, 1994). The longer your time-horizon, the more complexity you can deal with, the bigger the problems you can solve, and the more people you potentially can lead. Jaques's research has shown there are certain predictable break points, which he calls strata, at which the nature of capability changes dramatically, with the higher levels reflecting more complex thought patterns and being occupied by fewer and fewer individuals. Stratum I people have time-horizons of one day to three months into the future, IIs from three months to 1 year, IIIs from 1 to 2 years, IVs from 2 to 5 years, Vs from 5 to 10, VIs from 10 to 20 years, and VIIs from 20 to 50 years. The extraordinarily rare VIIIs and above, who think huge, very complex, ground-breaking thoughts, have time-horizons of 50 to 100 years or more into the future (Jaques and Cason, 1994).

Because the percentage of people occupying the higher strata is progressively smaller than the percentage in the lower ones, another plausible explanation I have heard for SST's relative anonymity is that only those with capabilities in Strata V through VIII can truly understand SST. Given the low proportion of the big, visionary thinkers who occupy those strata, it will take a sizable amount of time to accumulate a critical mass of individuals who both comprehend Jaques's work and have the capability to put it into practice.

On the surface, this is a persuasive argument; and if one happens to suffer from a touch of vanity, it is particularly attractive to those whose capability is in Strata V through VIII. Persuasive as the argument may be, I have concluded from my experience that neither our under-standing of SST nor our acceptance or rejection of its es-sence is related to capability, as long as our capability is located in what Jaques terms "the normal adult range" of Strata I through VIII (Jaques, 1989).

For example, I know a Stratum VI colleague who, with temples throbbing, has vehemently rejected SST, employing abstract "arguments supported by accumulated conceptual information in which the concepts are actually related to each other" (Jaques, 1990a). My colleague contends that SST is fascistic in its underlying value system, violates Kant-ian moral imperatives, and is based on flawed scientific methodology. Consequently, he has concluded that SST's resulting gestalt is both scientifically and morally unaccept-able as a theoretical model for conceptualizing organiza-tional behavior. Although I don't agree with either his premises or his conclusions, I do realize that the thought process by which he reached them is an expression of what those of us at the lower strata of Jaques's Universal Depth Structure (1976) would consider to be in the upper reaches of capability.

Alternatively, I have heard Stratum I individuals, who live and work in the "World of Concrete Language and Ideas" (Jaques, 1990b), embrace SST with simple, uncom-plicated assertive statements, such as "You can piss all over the guy's work if you want to, but he is right. It makes sense to me. I like what he says. It's great stuff."

In short, once acquainted with the fundamentals of SST, whether by reading or through conversation with someone knowledgeable about the subject, everyone understands the theory, even though the specific nature of each individual's understanding undoubtedly varies as a function of the capability he or she brings to the task.

Examining that conclusion retrospectively, I don't know why I, or anyone else for that matter, should be surprised by it. Jaques, for one, has discovered that people both can and will discuss potentially complex issues such as euthanasia, abortion, or any other subject that interests them, within the limits set by their own capability (Jaques, 1990b). In fact, one can judge others' capability from the structure of thought they employ as they discuss such topics. Or, to provide a slightly different example: all of us understand the Bible, assuming we bother to read it; how we interpret its content and whether we accept or reject what we understand from reading it is an entirely different matter. Apparently, that is true for our comprehension of elephants, also. That we can discuss elephants in our own unique ways that reflect our respective levels of inborn capability doesn't provide a clue as to which of us will like or dislike having an elephant padding around in our parlors. For reasons that Jaques's theory doesn't explain, one person's elephant droppings are another's organic fertilizer.

The Implications of SST Are Unclear

Initially, I entertained the possibility that the spread of SST might be limited because its practical implications were unclear. To the contrary, I have discovered that if anything, the spread of SST has been restricted because its practical implications *are* clear.

For example, I know a human resources (HR) manager who permitted forty-eight hundred hourly employees to go on strike rather than employ SST as a conceptual guide for resolving a labor-management dispute. He did so even though he believed that the dispute clearly related to the organization's failure to provide Felt-Fair Pay and to the anti-requisite accountability relationships that existed between the organization's Stratum II first-line managers and its Stratum I hourly employees.

Paradoxically, the HR manager refused to use SST not because he feared it would not work but because he feared it *would*. According to him, SST's success would open up a Pandora's box of issues relating to the organization's basic structure, its compensation scheme, and the managerial and quasimanagerial roles played by specific organizational members. Most of all, it would call into question a lot of activities that went on in his own area of organizational accountability. In his words, "I'd rather call in a traditional organizational development consultant to do a good ol' intergroup conflict resolution design, even though I know that type of intervention won't solve the problems we have.[1] At least others around here would think we were trying to do something, and I wouldn't run the risk of being the focus of a lot of downstream flap I couldn't control if this SST stuff caught on."

Although I might question both his ethics and his business judgment for choosing a nonsolution that he knew wouldn't work instead of a solution that he believed might work, I think he was essentially correct in assessing the potential ripple effect the theory might have had on him and the remainder of the organization. To him, the implications of the theory were crystal clear, and that clarity led him to reject its use. Some might say he was resistant to change. I would say he didn't want to suffer from the anaclitic depression blues that might follow the successful application of a new theoretical approach to solving his organization's problems.

In similar fashion, I have been approached by more than one director of an executive development program for which I have been scheduled to do a presentation about SST's potential for draining the environmental swamps that produce organizational phrog farms (Harvey, 1988c), with a question such as, "Talking about phrog farming is risky enough, but must you speak about SST? Couldn't you do a session on something else?" When I have asked the reason for their queries, their replies generally have been versions of, "The implications of SST to the participants are too disturbing. They will get to thinking that a lot of what goes on in their own organizations doesn't make much sense. And, more important to me, it means that a lot of the other material in the program dealing with leadership style, organization structure, compensation, conflict resolution, empowerment, the role of personality in management, career development, motivation, strategic planning, and management development won't make much sense, either. It also causes a problem for future presenters who speak on those topics, not to mention the headaches it creates for me when the participants start complaining about the contradictions between SST and most of the other material we provide."

When I ask, "Would you prefer that I present some additional material that doesn't make sense so that it would fit both the nonsensical organizational environments of the participants and the nonsensical material of the program?" they generally have said, "No, but I thought I would ask. I just don't like the implications of Jaques's work, even though his ideas are extremely interesting and, undoubtedly, represent a real advance in the field."

Nor is their attitude significantly different from that voiced by a doctoral student who took a course that I not*teach and in which *A General Theory of Bureaucracy* and *Human Capability* are used as textbooks. During the course, the elephant himself occasionally wanders around and bangs against the classroom's walls as a guest professor. Several years after the doctoral student took the course, she visited my office to discuss some of her experiences.

"Do you still use Elliott Jaques's book, and does he still serve as a guest speaker from time to time?" she asked.

"The answer is 'yes' to both questions," I replied. "Why do you ask?"

"I hated the book, and when he spoke to our class, I was very upset by nearly everything he said."

"Would you mind telling me why?"

"Well, if he's correct, and I suspect that he is, then much of the material I've received in my doctoral program about how school systems should be organized and about the way in which people learn is probably irrelevant. I feel like a large part of my time as a doctoral student has been wasted."

"Well, if you believe that, why don't you just forget about Jaques's work and 'dance with the one that brung you'?" I replied, using a Texas expression that means "stick with the concepts and theories with which you were previously familiar."

"I can't," she said. "Doing that would be like trying to sit in the corner, on command, for thirty seconds without thinking about a brown bear."

Evidently, elephants sometimes develop thick coats of fur and replace their tusks with fangs.

The Theoretical Relationships Proposed by SST Would Not Hold Up in the World of Practice

A final explanation I have heard for the relatively limited spread of SST is that its basic theoretical constructs would not be validated if individuals attempted to apply them in their respective organizations. Although I have heard variations of that argument a number of times, I have never heard it offered by people who actually have experimented with SST in their organizations. In the light of such data, I see no reason to pursue that point of view further. More specifically, until someone tells me or you or Jaques or some other verifiable source that he has had an experience with an actual (rather than a hypothetical) managerial accountability hierarchy in which Time Span of Discretion is not reliably related to Felt-Fair Pay; human capability does not follow predictable developmental courses; and living, breathing human beings with Stratum IV capabilities have effective work relationships, as subordinates, with Stratum

III superiors, I see no need to worry about the elephant's health.

Having rejected five seemingly plausible explanations for why so many people who should be familiar with—even if not necessarily in agreement with—SST are not, I turn the discussion now to what I think are the true reasons for SST's limited dissemination and the collateral question, "Who the hell is Elliott Jaques?"

SST as a New Expression from the World of Universals

In my opinion, SST is not merely a technological prescription for analyzing and constructing economically efficient associations and accountability hierarchies, although it certainly is useful for that purpose. Nor is it simply a methodological guide for enhancing organizational design or improving our understanding and practice of organizational leadership and management. Rather, using Jaques's terms, SST is an expression of encompassing "Universal" thoughts that are generated by those very rare big thinkers who come from Stratum VIII and above (Jaques and Cason, 1994). These are the individuals who describe and develop universal ideas, languages, theories, values, and concepts that are required for handling whole societies, social movements, ideologies, and philosophies (Jaques, 1990b).

Like all new theories generated by these people, SST requires that those of us in the field of organizational behavior either change or abandon many of our cherished, established beliefs about the nature of human organization. In addition, it requires that we either change or abandon our relationships with friends and colleagues who have supported us in holding such outdated beliefs.

In short, SST demands that we abandon not only the systems of thought but also the isomorphic networks of associates that have provided us with the emotional security we derive from maintaining those systems. Such changes, in turn, would cause many (and maybe most) of us to suffer from those anaclitic depression blues, which, as you know, is a form of depression that strikes otherwise normal individuals when the emotional support provided by other people, familiar belief systems, or organizational structures is withdrawn. As you know from Chapter Six, if anaclitic depression runs its full course, it results in marasmus—a type of debilitating atrophy that can be both physical and emotional in nature; and because of that, most of us fear the anaclitic depression blues and will take whatever actions we can to avoid it.

Thus, like the alchemists, who were threatened with obsolescence by the emerging theory of chemistry, many of us associated with the field of organizational behavior probably have attempted to avoid the experience of anaclitic depression by ignoring SST and continuing to live in the thin atmosphere of false security supplied by a theoretical environment with which we are comfortably familiar.[2] As I described many years ago in an organizational sermon titled "OD as a Religious Movement" (Harvey, 1974), we are singing our own version of the traditional hymn: "Give me that old time religion, Give me that old time religion, Give me that old time religion, It's good enough for me."

Paradoxically, the fact that many of us have lived much of our lives in organizations that generate, rather than ameliorate, anaclitic depression doesn't help us withstand the fear of separation, abandonment, or ostracism that the threat of anaclitic depression poses for us. Experience, in many cases, is not the best teacher. At times, it may be the worst.

Fundamentally new ideas (SST being one) emanating from those who occupy the strata of Universals inevitably require us to engage in the kind of intense debate and controversy that frequently leads to strained and fractured interpersonal relationships, resulting in the anaclitic depression blues. I am convinced, therefore, that our fear of experiencing the blues has stifled the discussion, dissemination, and development of SST itself, even though it offers a potential organizational blueprint for gaining existential relief from the anaclitic depression of which we are so afraid.

Strange, isn't it? Parlor-reared elephants apparently activate whatever self-defeating proclivities we human beings inherently possess.

One is then forced to ask, "From whence comes the impetus for any fundamental change in the way of seeing or experiencing the world? Why would anyone embark on the development of a heretofore unexpressed idea, such as SST, if our inherent fear of those anaclitic blues is so great?"

Once more, SST offers a fecund hint. Perhaps individuals with capability in the Universal range are in touch with the truth and reality of the Universal ideas themselves; perhaps they receive emotional support and gain reassurance from their contact with and attachment to these ideas, ideas that have no reality and provide no security to those of us whose capability is lower. For instance, "$e = mc^2$" may have given Einstein a lot of emotional support and reassurance, but that piece of esoteric scribbling would have said absolutely nothing that provided comfort, reassurance, and security for me.

Jaques's Major Potential Contribution: A Means for Elucidating and Clarifying Ethical, Moral, and Spiritual Issues of Organization

Assuming that SST does emanate from the world of Universals, I doubt that its major contribution will stem from the practical, technological guidelines it provides for creating requisite accountability hierarchies, associations, and other forms of organization. Rather, I believe it will come from SST's capacity for providing a more sophisticated, rigorous order of concepts and language for illuminating the kind of ethical, moral, and spiritual (EMS) relationships that we human beings require both to survive and to flourish in a wide variety of organizations. It will do so, I believe, because new Universal statements—which by their nature require that we restructure interpersonal, organizational, and intellectual alliances—*always* demand isomorphic changes in EMS relationships within and among persons whose capabilities are found in the lower strata.

For example, SST has led me to understand that the empirical relationship that exists between Felt-Fair Pay and Time Span of Discretion is not simply the basis of a reliable technique for determining monetary compensation schedules in accountability hierarchies. Rather, it also serves as an invitation for me, and others, to consider rigorously how we express fairness and unfairness, decency and indecency, support and rejection, respect and disrespect, love and hate, kindness and cruelty, competence and incompetence, greed and altruism toward one another through the medium of compensation.

Or, by making me aware of the potential isomorphic relationship that exists between a given individual's capability and the complexity of work she is capable of carrying out, SST demands that I explore the EMS issues that arise when we create organizations in which this relationship is either facilitated or inhibited. For instance, what EMS issues stem from giving individuals work that is below or above their capability? More specifically, I am convinced that profound EMS issues are raised when we give people

How Come Every Time I Get Stabbed in the Back My Fingerprints Are on the Knife?

work at a level that bores or overwhelms them to death; and SST clearly shows us how to keep from doing that.

Or, knowing the predictable course of a given individual's development of capability over time, I am equipped with a new way of thinking about the EMS issues that are related to the education of our young, our middle-aged, and our elderly. What EMS issues are involved, for instance, when we make the rather common but false assumption that virtually all students of the same age are on the same developmental trajectory of capability? If you know SST, you will understand why grouping students on the basis of capability, not age, may facilitate their ethical, moral, and spiritual development.

Or, employing SST as a conceptual guide, and assuming that we succeed in creating an organization based on SST, I must ask whether it is ethically, morally, or spiritually legitimate for me and others to hoard our knowledge of SST and, by doing so, gain a competitive advantage over poorly designed organizations for the purpose of diminishing their relative effectiveness or destroying them.

Or, playing with the implications of SST's constructs in depth, I am led to conclude that an organization's structure can be moral or immoral in and of itself. Thus I realize that consciously constructing an organization that, by its design, impairs people's health is ultimately no different than willfully using asbestos in the construction of a brick-and-mortar building when we know that the material is likely to compromise the health of the building's inhabitants.

I suspect that knowledge of SST will likewise arouse EMS issues in you and others, the specific character of which undoubtedly will reflect your respective capabilities. In addition, I know that discussions of issues dealing with right and wrong, or good and evil, inevitably generate intense controversies, the exploration of which may result in broken relationships that lead to the anaclitic depression blues. Given the dangers involved, we may be very reticent to engage in those types of exploration. Jaques himself may have fallen victim to such reticence. For instance, in *A General Theory of Bureaucracy* (1976), *Free Enterprise, Fair Employment* (1982), and *Requisite Organization* (1989), he has discussed a variety of ethical and moral implications of SST at the individual, organizational, and political levels, but he, for the most part, has refrained from exploring the deeper spiritual implications of his work.

Assuming that both he and those of us who are stimulated by his ideas overcome our fears of the anaclitic depression blues and develop the intellectual, collegial, and transcendent attachments required to explore the ethical, moral, and spiritual implications of SST, I don't think that many individuals in the organizational behavior field will be asking one another, "Who the hell is Elliott Jaques?" Rather, the next time the CEO invites us for cocktails in his spacious Manhattan penthouse, I think many of us will find ourselves earnestly puzzling over the question, "How the hell could so many of us fail to notice the pachyderm in the parlor?"

CHAPTER NINE

On Tooting Your Own Horn or Social Intervention as the Process of Releasing Flatus in the Confines of Religious Institutions

Bobby Lee Bemus
Blue Point University, Blue Point, Texas
(as told to Jerry B. Harvey)

Musing with Professor Harvey about elephants in parlors led me in a peculiar direction. Specifically, it caused me to think about how the generic issues relating to the nature and effectiveness of social intervention, regardless of the specific interventionist and regardless of the social system in which the intervention occurs, are analogous to releasing flatus in the confines of religious institutions.

You might think that the subject of such contemplation is rather odd, particularly for one who is certified neither as a medical doctor nor as a theologian. I can honestly say, however, that I have gotten inspiration for my thoughts from an atmosphere of inquiry fermented by the exploits of Lukey Ledbetter, a lifetime acquaintance, a sometime friend, and the focus of a volatile debate within our Church. The story of Lukey, his role in the conflagration, and the implications I draw from his activities for understanding the process of social intervention are aired for your consideration and possible inspiration. At worst, the discussion may be suffocating. At best, it might turn out to be a breath of fresh air.

The Lukey Ledbetter Story

To begin with, Lukey Ledbetter is gone, and I suppose about the kindest thing I can say is that those of us who were close to him are unclear as to how we feel about his passing. I know for sure that some folks actually cheered, although I must say for the sake of historical and scientific accuracy that I personally didn't hear an awful lot of that. I know for certain that a few—Miss Lucille Tate being a prime example—voiced a lot of regrets. I also talked with others who had tears in their eyes when we spoke of Lukey, but I have the distinct feeling that many of those responded more as crocodiles than as true mourners. I suppose I could cover my tracks best if I would just say that Lukey's passing generated genuine ambivalence.

One school of thought stoutly contends that Lukey still attends services but does so in some sort of disguise. Knowing people around here as I do, and being more than somewhat familiar with Lukey and his ways, I rather doubt that. Someone would have sniffed him out by now. Lukey never was much for maintaining the subtleties that a caper of that sort would require.

With all the steam that's been generated, a clear-headed soul can only wonder what will happen when he dies.

Now that I've gotten this far, I suddenly realize that you may not altogether comprehend the nuances of what I'm

How Come Every Time I Get Stabbed in the Back My Fingerprints Are on the Knife?

saying, because you likely aren't acquainted with Lukey. Likewise, you may not be a full-fledged member of the Church. Or it may be because you *do* know Lukey and *are* a member of the Church that your comprehension, like mine, is somewhat confused or maybe altogether lacking.

So let me see if I can get right to the point, ethereal as that point may be. For as long as I can remember, Lukey's passing was a source of controversy among us in the congregation. You see, since the age of eight, Lukey Ledbetter, who is unmarried, forty-four, paunchy, and slightly balding, played a unique role in the Church's affairs. Specifically, like T. J. Lambert, the infamous defensive end of the New York Giants, Lukey possessed the rare capacity to pass gas at will (Jenkins, 1973).

Ask him for a long slow one, and he could deliver it. Or if you wanted a short sweet one, he could lay it right on you. In the tradition of Le Petomane, the amazing turn-of-the-century Parisian artist who "breezed his way to fame and fortune" at the Moulin Rouge (Nohain and Caradee, 1985, book jacket), Lukey could play simple tunes. Those who know him well will swear on the Good Book that he could produce them in all colors of the rainbow. According to his cousin Leroy, Lukey could even peel the paint off the walls, right down to the original layer of an authentic colonial house, but would do so only if the situation clearly called for it. To the best of my knowledge, no one around here has had the nerve to ask Leroy for a precise description of the conditions that were required to provoke Lukey to such extraordinary outpourings of his talent, although more than one of us have speculated at length from time to time about the answer to that question.

Let it be said that when Lukey opted to intervene in the life of the Church, most demeaned his interventions as overblown. Others hailed them as sources of genuine inspiration. Several of the latter persons, who also belong to the local literary club, buttressed their opinions with the rather provocative observation, "If Martin Luther was correct in contending that you can destroy the devil by passing gas directly into his nostrils [Erikson, 1972], then Lukey must have been a special conduit of God's Natural Gas and Pipeline Company."

As one might guess, given the atmosphere that surrounded him, Lukey was a source of awe, disgust, respect, controversy, laughter, derision, and joy, depending on whom in the congregation you approached. But of him few could have been said to have no opinion, because above all, Lukey was the subject of constant conversation and many rich stories. Most of those stories were recounted in meetings of the Joy Seekers, the Church's governing board. (According to their charter, the Joy Seekers were formed as a result of the women's Joy council coupling with the men's Seekers council for the purpose of producing a more joyful world. But that is altogether another story, the recitation of which could serve only to detract from your understanding of Lukey's story.)

Lukey's exploits were legendary. Few members, from the smallest toddler to the elderly Cecil Goodman, cannot remember at least one occasion when a Bach oratorio, which was being rendered inert by Madame Delray Skulley (our rather pretentious and untalented soprano), was transformed into a version of the *1812 Overture* as the staccato products of Lukey's Saturday night forays to the Alamo Taco Parlor burst forth like muted cannon shots and reverberated around the church's vaulted ceilings. Captain Roscoe Danner (Ret.), our congregation's esteemed historian, has been heard on more than one occasion to remark that Lukey's incursions into the field of music criticism consistently conjured up fond memories of artillery barrages he experienced during his long and distinguished career as a professional peace keeper.

Likewise, it is difficult to find a parishioner who cannot recount, some with barely contained glee, a time when a major point of one of the Reverend August Dinwittie's sonorous, portentous, and sometimes pompous sermons was punctuated—or deflated—by one of Lukey's acclamations to the ethereal spirits that expressed the essence of his soul.

Some of Lukey's exploits have been inflated by rumor, puffed by exaggeration, and expanded by repetition until they have become permanent features of the Church's folklore—their permanence approximating that of the marble columns supporting the balconies that provided a haven for those stolid soldiers of the Church who sought shelter and relief from the great undeclared war emanating from the pews below.

Some key parishioners, Miss Lucille Tate being their chief spokesperson, vehemently and indignantly contend that the stained glass windows that have long adorned each side of the sanctuary are not the product of the esteemed

Teutonic craftsman to whom they were attributed in the rusted time capsule rescued from the weathered cornerstone during the Church's centennial celebration, but rather are the end results of Lukey's unique approach to religious expression.

Until recently, despite his controversial role, Lukey apparently remained blithely untouched, unperturbed, and uninfluenced by the uproar, the tension, the deprecation, and the occasional approbation that his interventions in the life of the Church created. In response to what most members euphemistically called a Lukey Special, the Joy Seekers could fervently pray for his redemption or Old Man Goodman could mutter an equally earnest "good show" and the effect on Lukey appeared to be the same. As Bobby Joe Minter so aptly put it, "Some people step to the beat of their own drummers, but Lukey seemed to prefer following the base horn player."

Whatever the source of his sacerdotal guidance, until recently I think that all parishioners—friends, foes, and fence-sitters alike—would say unequivocally that Lukey possessed spiritual vitality and was a volatile force to be reckoned with.

I say "until recently" because Lukey's exploits seem to have come to an end. More precisely, he apparently has fallen from grace and the redemptive qualities of his efforts to help both him and us cope with life's indigestible demands have been replaced by the bitter acid of bile. I am sad. The Reverend Mr. Dinwittie is sad. The congregation is sad. Even more important, the spirit of dejection pervades Lukey himself. On those rare occasions when he attends services, he sits passively, quietly, with a depressed look of bloated resignation knowing that his position of importance in the Church's affairs has been lost and that the aura of notoriety and respect with which he once was held is no more. His spiritual deflation is all encompassing. Consequently, both he and we know, though none of us has come right out and said it straight on, that it is only a matter of time before he shifts his membership to another church, if he decides to attend a church at all, and if any church will have him.

As best I can tell, his fall occurred not because he abused his privilege—some would say his inalienable right—to use his unusual skill to change the atmosphere of the Church as the spirit moved him. Rather, he made the mistake of trying to convince others to join him in doing so, contending that others not only could but *should* express their spiritual essences by using the outlet he so masterfully employed.

The specific event that led to Lukey's deflation occurred on the day the Most Reverend Mr. Dinwittie chose as his topic of metaphysical sustenance the rather challenging sobriquet "This, too, shall pass." As the announcement of the sermon selection rolled from the good reverend's flaccid lips, a noise that some interpreted as a sonic boom and others as an explosion of our ancient boiler rattled the hallowed edifice from its foundations to its spires.

When it became apparent to the Reverend Mr. Dinwittie and those of us in the congregation that the Concorde's flight pattern did not include Blue Point and that the church's ancient boiler would live to serve yet another day, we instinctively turned to Lukey, the one other potential source of disruption upon whom we could faithfully rely. Knowing that Lukey was prone to carminative outbursts when confronted with what he considered to be clichés, it was with relief—but not surprise—that we saw his wry, knowing smile that indicated, without a doubt, that he had brought the full force of his unique skill to bear on our esteemed pastor's attempts to cope with the same invisible devils that generated Lukey's spiritual dyspepsia.

We were prepared for Lukey's outburst and for the loud guffaw that was quickly transformed into a rasping cough by Brother Goodman, who wasn't exactly a fan of banality, either. We were prepared for the look on Miss Lucille Tate's countenance, a look of pious resignation as, with eyes cocked toward the stained glass windows in the upper reaches of the church's massive sanctuary, she gasped ever so slightly and covered her mouth with the ever-present embroidered handkerchief that she plucked from the sleeve of her lace-trimmed dress. We knew we could count on her leading the Joy Seekers in a ritual prayer seeking either Lukey's redemption or destruction. We also knew she wisely would leave the ultimate decision of which course of action to follow to the One Great Interventionist who the Joy Seekers believed legitimately could act on their behalf.

How Come Every Time I Get Stabbed in the Back My Fingerprints Are on the Knife?

We were also prepared for the manner in which Elrod Fenton, the town's pharmacist who sat in the pew directly in front of Lukey, reacted in his usual, predictable fashion by suddenly disappearing from his seat and dropping to the floor as if searching for some minute object. We knew that the object would never be found, since it never existed. Nevertheless, we were willing to play our part in his benign deception, because we also knew where the good air lay.

We were not prepared, however, for the wry, knowing, yet uneasy look of guilt-ridden relief, chiseled as if it were a living memorial to Lukey and his skills, on the face of Claude Wilkens, Lukey's longtime friend and Taco Parlor companion.

It took only a moment for us to realize that we had suffered a simultaneous attack from two sources, only one of which we had expected. We were not prepared for that. In fact, we reacted as if we had been threatened by two mad bombers.

Had Claude's contribution been a chance occurrence, I don't think much would have come of the whole episode in the long run. Life is full of surprises, and the fortuitous pairing of the flatus response could have been one of them. But, to our dismay, this was not the case.

Our suspicions were aroused during the subsequent weekly meetings of the Joy Seekers, when it became abundantly clear that the tandem barrage was not solely the product of God's providential will but rather the premeditated product of Lukey's conversion and training of his old friend Claude.

The evidence that led to our conclusion was vaporous, at best, so it was not easy to gather. In fact, it took several months; but by then it was convincing.

One Saturday night, Billy Ray Coleman and his wife, Vada Sue, saw Lukey and Claude having a late evening enchilada dinner at the Alamo Taco Parlor. Nita Lee Pomroy, the waitress, allowed as to how a number of customers sitting in the area of the table occupied by Lukey and Claude had left prior to completing their pralines; they complained that they were suffering from what they termed "Alamo Asthma." According to Ms. Pomroy, she first thought that the disease really existed, since the exodus was led by the town's physician, Dr. Cletus Moses, who had both identified the disease and, amid much laughter, pointed to Lukey and Claude as the carriers. Eventually, Ms. Roland "put the cap on the stack" when she reported that she had overheard Lukey tell Claude, "Claude, I've decided that for your own good you've got to learn to toot your horn like me. And I'm a-gonna teach you how." Later, she said that the conversation smelled fishy to her because, as she put it, "I knew for sure those boys didn't play in no band."

Well, one thing led to another, and before we knew it, the chair of the Joy Seekers met eyeball-to-eyeball with Lukey and confronted him with the question, "Lukey, did you or did you not egg ol' Claude into passing gas in church?" Lukey replied with what I thought at the time was admirable candor, "You bet. And I'm a-gonna work on Ol'

214

Man Goodman next. The climate of the church needs changing, and, with a little help, I think I can do it. If I can get Claude and Ol' Man Goodman to go along, I think the three of us might even convince the Reverend Mr. Dinwittie to cut a few capers himself. With the pastor himself on our side, we would have it made. The four of us might even smoke ol' Elrod off the floor."

To this day, no one knows for sure what got into Lukey that led him to do what he did. Nadine Bostick, who had taken some night courses in philosophy at the college, said she was positive that some fellow named Husserl would say that Lukey missed the transcendental turn and embarked upon an evangelical bent. We didn't pay much attention to her because, in the first place, we didn't understand what she said. In the second place, not one of us was acquainted with her friend Mr. Husserl, and we had enough trouble in the Church without running the risk of interference from someone who might turn out to cause as much ferment as Lukey. No matter what that foreigner, Mr. Husserl, had to say, everyone involved knew for sure that something more than tacos must have led to Lukey's mysterious transformation. Regardless of what that "something" was, the Joy Seekers decided that Lukey's pronouncement of ecclesiastical intent clearly produced more flatus within the confines of our beloved Church than the institution could bear. Consequently, they led a movement that resulted in Lukey's being censured during a tumultuous debate among the congregation as a whole. In the end, being censured completely drained Lukey of his heretofore indomitable spirit, and his fate was sealed.

Searching for
Redeeming Features

Since, for all intents and purposes, the Lukey we knew and loved—and detested—is gone and Ol' Claude has shrunk into chastened silence, I've decided to see if I can make the best of an otherwise bad situation and find some redeeming features to the whole saga. I was stumped for a long time as to how to go about it. Then, the other night, as I munched on a Taco Parlor burrito while preparing a lecture for my class on organizational consultation, I came upon a homily by Brother Chris Argyris, a secular preacher on the Organizational Development Gospel Circuit. According to Brother Argyris, "To intervene is to enter into an ongoing system of relationships, to come between or among persons, groups or objects for the purpose of helping them" (1970, p. 15).

I suddenly realized that Lukey, whatever you might think of what he did, or whether you believed it was helpful or not, was one of the most competent, and incompetent, interventionists I'd ever run across. Consequently, I decided to do a little philosophizing about the relationship between releasing flatus in the confines of religious institutions and the process of social intervention in general.

Although you may reach other conclusions, I summarize the substance of mine below, in no particular order of importance. They are more the end products of a stream of consciousness than anything else.

Some Thoughts on the Relationship Between Social Intervention and the Process of Releasing Flatus in the Confines of Religious Institutions

1. Social intervention always involves the introduction of a new system of behavior, based on different values, into an ongoing social process. The impact of such a value-laden intervention frequently is disconcerting because it brings our own values into account. Sometimes the intervention strengthens our values, and sometimes it leads us to realize that they are, as my grandmother used to say, of no account whatsoever.

2. If an intervention coincides with our values, we honor it with such names as psychotherapy, consultation, leadership, social work, group facilitation, preaching, whistle blowing, parenting, or patriotic revolution. If it doesn't, we disparage it by calling it head shrinking, robbery by Beltway Bandits, demagoguery, governmental interference, manipulation, indoctrination, meddling, rabble rousing, child abuse, or terrorism. Regardless of the appellation we assign to it, an intervention by any other name is still an intervention.

3. The position we take in response to any particular social intervention is both transparent and predictable once you know where we stand, or sit, in relation to the values involved. For example, I have noticed that the amount of approbation we members of the Church accord interventionists is correlated directly with the distance we are from them as they go about their work. Parishioners who sat in the relative safety of the church balcony consistently expressed the most admiration for Lukey and his escapades. It was only when Lukey arrived late and had to sit by them that they got agitated.

4. Most members of a social system secretly respect people who possess the skill for social intervention and who exercise it with unaffected gusto. Similar to the way we balcony-sitters made an effort to keep from associating too closely with Lukey and his ways, and even though we did not openly admit our admiration for him, deep down, we frequently wished we had the capacity to emulate him. Like our patriot forbearers, almost all of us long to fire at least one good shot that will be heard 'round the world—whatever the nature of that world might be. When you get right down to it, most of us have patriotic spirits.

5. Social intervention is a natural, organic process, although I am sure its nuances can be developed and honed through disciplined study and practice. As best I can tell it's a self-preserving reaction of an organism to some sort of potentially destructive disequilibrium. Consequently, those who choose to develop and use

whatever capacity they have for it are more comfortable and healthy in the long run than those who don't.
If you believe in Darwin, you might even conclude that
the process has long-term survival value. In fact, individuals and organizations that are in a state of ferment and
don't practice social intervention likely will share the fate
of the dinosaurs.

Maybe that's what is really being discussed when
you read in the newspaper that a high-ranking executive was destroyed by pressure, that a neighborhood ex-
ploded in rage, or that a volatile situation exists in one
of those heathen countries where missionaries to the
Church have tried to intervene. At the very broadest
level, the Big Bang Theory—which learned experts here
at the college say explains the creation of our universe—
may represent nothing more than God's reaction to a
pressure-filled day at His, or Her, office.

6. Some of us have more inborn capacity for engaging
in social intervention than others. However, like Lukcy,
who never was invited to join any of the important com-
mittees of the Church and who was never a true blue Joy
Seeker, the ones with the greatest capacities tend to live
on the periphery of the Church and its activities.

7. Competent social interventionists express reality
in an uncompromising way. Blue Point's only psychoanalyst, Dr. Wilfred Bion (1970), who must have been
a blood relative of Lukey and who was known for his
extraordinary skill as an interventionist, contends that
any social system will die if it doesn't constantly strive

to live within the limits that reality provides. Furthermore, Dr. Bion says that the primary task of any interventionist worth his burrito is to provide others with an experience of that reality. In fact, according to the good doctor Bion, sharing reality in an uncompromising way is the only way we can avoid living in a fantasy world that destroys ourselves and others.

8. Competent interventionists are a constant source of stimulation, tension, and excitement. For instance, I know for certain that attendance picked up whenever we knew Lukey was going to be in Church. Even his detractors showed up out of fear they might miss an occasion worth detracting about. For those of us who live lives of quiet desperation while worshiping at the Church's altar, people like Lukey provide a source of welcome vicarious relief. As Sister Tate so poetically observed, "Although he may not have been the most popular member of the congregation, everybody got a bang out of him."

Regardless of Sister Tate's observation, however, when it comes to the process of intervening, vicarious relief is never as satisfying as the real thing. Stated differently, it is always more enjoyable to be the agent of change than to be an observer or the target of change. Simply observing becomes uninteresting pretty quickly, and being a target that is shot at never is much fun, regardless of the circumstances.

9. You might say that tension and excitement have a paradoxical way of bringing everyone, even enemies, together. Old Man Goodman and Elrod weren't the best of

How Come Every Time I Get Stabbed in the Back My Fingerprints Are on the Knife?

friends under any circumstances, but they clearly made an effort to communicate when the topic of Lukey came to the fore.

10. Competent interventionists are frequently offensive but seldom obscene. Even the learned members of the Supreme Court haven't been able to do much about telling us when the line separating one from the other is crossed. However, the Reverend Mr. Dinwittie came close to it for me in one of his sermons when he said, "If any of the great prophets were alive today, they would be out pumping gas, not sitting around in some plushy office telling others to do it for them. They would be service station attendants, not managers of marketing."

I'm sure that many in our congregation thought Rev. Mr. Dinwittie's statement might have been offensive, but I doubt if any thought it was obscene. I know for sure that it was one of the few times I ever heard Lukey employ his vocal cords to say "amen."

11. The core of every so-called healthy Church is made up of Joy Seekers. Although they may have many other names, they are the pillars of the Church; their primary purpose is to support the powerful structures that are required to absorb, deflect, or otherwise contain the explosive potential of competent interventionists.

12. Regardless of the structures they confront, competent social interventionists ultimately clear the air rather than pollute it. Lukey, for instance, seldom got wind of what went on when the Joy Seekers met. When he did,

221

though, he sure didn't store it within himself for safe keeping, or more to the point, for keeping safe. Rather, he went to them, regularly as the evening breeze, and passed whatever wind may have blown his way in an act of natural confrontation that left many of the Joy Seekers looking as if they wanted to expire. Paradoxically, his breeziness also resulted in what a few of the participants called a refreshing change of climate.

13. After hearing the latter comment from more than one member of the Joy Seekers, I now have a new appreciation for the real meaning of the everyday statement, "We are caught in the winds of change." I also have a lot of sympathy for those who are being captured.

14. Having been around Lukey when he was on the firing line, I also have comprehended for the first time why virtually all competent interventionists have reputations for being "straight shooters."

15. Competent interventionists base their interventions more on the faith that spiritual conviction provides than on calculations of the effect their interventions might have on themselves and others. Knowing that, I more fully comprehend what another competent social interventionist, Mother Teresa, had in mind when she said, "We are not called upon to be successful, but to be faithful" (Sham, 1997, p. 17A).

Using Mother Teresa and the early Lukey as models, I have an uncomfortable feeling that the ultimate question facing all interventionists is whether the faith that undergirds their interventions is based on anything of transcendent importance. I am sure about the transcendent nature of the faith that supported Mother Teresa's interventions; however, I do have doubts about the nature of the faith that undergirds the work of many interventionists. When Lukey got into trouble at the Taco Parlor, my doubts extended to him no less than many others.

16. Understanding the important role of transcendence in the intervention process, I am sure that competent interventionists never distribute reaction forms or conduct public opinion polls to ascertain the value of their interventions. In fact, any time I hear interventionists ask for feedback as a means of providing themselves with guidance for future interventions, I know that their competence is limited, and perhaps you feel the same way. Maybe that's one reason so many professional interventionists who base their interventions not on principled faith but on the results of such mechanisms as polls, ratings, feedback forms, and focus groups frequently leave us with queasy feelings in our stomachs. Such people are not intervening with new values; they are mirroring the values that are already present. They are not passing gas; they are inhaling smoke.

17. I suspect that the reputations of even the most competent interventionists frequently exceed the reality of their actual contributions, however important those contributions may be. Without doubt, Lukey in his early days was competent at what he did, but, effective as he was, he really didn't produce those magnificent stained glass windows in the sanctuary. That's a point I think that all interventionists would do well to remember, because interventionists who are otherwise competent inevitably get into trouble when they begin to believe the grandiose mythology that frequently springs up around them. In social intervention, as well as in life in general, a little hubris is a dangerous thing. That's why so many interventionists, Lukey included, get hoisted on their own petards.

18. I didn't realize how perfectly the phrase *hoisted on your own petard* fit Lukey and many other interventionists until I explored the origin of the word *petard* in Blue Point University's etymological dictionary. Historically, *petard* has variously been defined as "an explosive device formerly used to breach defenses," a "firecracker," and "to break wind." The phrase of itself came from the argot of World War I, when hand grenades were known as petards, and therefore means "to be blown up with one's own bomb" (Barnhart, 1995, p. 560).

All the rich meanings of *petard* and the rich metaphorical quality of the phrase in which it is so frequently employed seem to apply to Lukey and his escapades. He certainly employed an explosive device to breach others' defenses, and he ultimately got blown up by a bomb that undoubtedly belonged to him.

19. I wonder if interventionists ever have trouble tolerating themselves and their interventions? No matter how competent or incompetent they are, I'm pretty sure they do. After all, when their interventions are successful or when they backfire, the interventionists are engulfed by the same changes in climate they have attempted to create for others. Perhaps that explains why when you ask interventionists how life is going for them, it's not unusual to get the pungent reply, "It stinks."

20.   All forms of social expression have their natural limits. Thus, the explosive force of a lot of reality-oriented interventions produced by the Lukeys of this world dissipate rapidly when confronted by the Church's structural strength. Pillars of the Church and the structures they support are a lot stronger than one might think. They aren't called pillars of the Church without good reason.

This dissipation of energy, called *entropy,* is a phenomenon discovered by scientists interested in thermodynamics, a discipline that, among its many facets, includes the study of gases. Entropy may be another reason that so many interventionists, particularly those infected by hubris, complain of feeling empty, drained, exhausted, and out of gas. Burnout is rather common among interventionists who work in the Church. Knowing and accepting one's natural limits may be a good way to avoid it.

21.   Competent interventionists generally produce action and movement, although the specific form these take varies greatly. That's why it's more effective for an interventionist to provide inspiration for what others might do than have aspirations for what others should do. That way, no one gets needlessly disappointed.

22. Interventionists like Lukey get in real trouble when they try to convince others that they should join them in intervening. Some would say it's because others feel threatened and uncomfortable if the skill is widely shared. I, for one, don't believe that. Colleagues of mine who are experts in olfactory and auditory physiology tell me that if everyone exercised Lukey's approach to intervention in the Church, the new climate would be so commonplace that no one would be aware of it. Consequently, no one would find it disruptive. As one of my colleagues in the biology department said, "Fish are the last to know they are in water."

Others contend it's because candor and honesty don't pay. I'm sure Lukey had both thoughts, and for a time, so did I. But neither explanation makes much sense to me now. Rather, I think that trying to convince and then teach others to do something they may not want to do or may not need to do or may not have thought of doing is rather arrogant. Healthy, strong-willed people don't like it. I guess I think that may be where Lukey failed. Prose-lytizing has never been popular when matters of religion are concerned.

Interventionists also get in trouble when they decide to smoke out the Elrod Fentons of this world, forgetting that the Elrod Fentons have the right to choose the quality of the air they breathe, bad as the interventionists might judge that air to be. In fact, I think we would do well to remember that smoke itself is a pollutant and that

How Come Every Time I Get Stabbed in the Back My Fingerprints Are on the Knife?

trying to smoke others out is a fundamental error, if not an error of fundament.

I suppose I would summarize the whole saga of Lukey by saying that to be effective as an interventionist in any Church, you have to be content to toot your own horn and have faith that, if your music is good enough, others will join you in the chorus.

Epilogue

Yesterday was a turning point for our congregation. Lukey hadn't been around in a long time; and it was apparent to all concerned that, in his absence, something we treasured was missing, and I think we knew, deep down, what it was. The promise of good weather is no fun when the threat of thunder is forever removed. Dark clouds do have silver linings.

But then, at the close of a particularly lackluster sermon, the Reverend Mr. Dinwittie put forth his usual plaintive entreaty for those who wished to seek membership in the Church to join him at the front. His only taker was little Mae Belle Brimley. Nobody paid much attention until the moment when she stepped forward, twelve years old and pigtails swinging, to shake Rev. Mr. Dinwittie's outstretched hand. As their palms touched, the good reverend greeted her with an expression of banality that was extreme, even for him. "My dear, sweet, precious child, I can tell without any doubt whatsoever that you truly are one of Our Maker's most beloved little angels," he said in a tone of voice that would make saccharin seem downright bitter.

As the word *angels* soared from his mouth, Mae Belle's ankle-length skirt raised nearly imperceptibly and the innocent roar of lightning's companion reverberated once again throughout the hallowed halls. God, indeed, works in strange and mysterious ways.

The faces of the congregation came alive. Brother Goodman reached for his ear trumpet in an effort to verify what his wax-sealed ears had only hinted was true. Miss Lucille Tate plucked her embroidered handkerchief from the sleeve of her high-necked, lace-trimmed dress, breathed in quick tiny breaths, and covered the thin smile on her lips, as her eyes, brimming with tearful thanks, focused prayerfully on her beloved windows. Like a frightened prairie dog, Elrod Fenton disappeared once again under the pew. Even Rev. Mr. Dinwittie responded to the abrupt change in ecclesiastical climate and switched the closing hymn from "Throw Out the Lifeline" to "When the Trumpets of the Lord Shall Sound."

We were saved!

Mae Belle, we need you. Mae Belle, we love you. Please don't desert us. You are the stuff of which our hopes and dreams are made. Be a source of inspiration for us and, in return, as you face the stormy seas of life, may your sails always be full and your course forever downwind.

Amen!

About the Author

Bobby Lee Bemus is assistant professor of organizational behavior at Blue Point University. He recently received his Ph.D. there, where he scored an important breakthrough in higher education by narrating his dissertation to his doctoral committee rather than writing it. According to the committee's chair, "Bobby Lee could talk a fungus off a boxwood stump."

Since his graduation, Bemus has served as an interventionist for a number of different organizations in the Blue Point area. In addition, he has recounted several memorable articles in the fields of management and organization development. This is his first book chapter and his first collaborative effort with Dr. Harvey. He is divorced and resides in Blue, a suburb of Blue Point, where he regularly participates in the organizational activities of the Church.

CHAPTER TEN

Ode to Waco: When Bizarre Organizational Behavior Is Concerned, God Works in Strange and Mysterious Ways

Note: This chapter was written with Stephanie Lamberti.

I f you don't come out, we will bring you out."

"If you don't stay out, we will bring *you* out."

"I don't understand what you mean."

"I don't understand what *you* mean."

"By whose authority do you act?"

"The God of Seven Seals. By whose authority do *you* act?"

"The God of the Single Seal pictured in the flag behind my desk."

"Your god is a false god."

"No, *your* god is a false god."

"But under the direction of your god you killed ten of our people."

"Under the direction of *your* god you killed four of ours."

"Before you say anything else, we killed yours because you were abusing your women and children."

"No, we killed yours because *you* were abusing our women and children."

"Anyone who thinks the way you do is totally insane."

"Anyone who thinks the way *you* do is totally insane."

"As proof of your insanity, we are going to surround you with the sounds of rabbits being slaughtered and then smash your house down with tanks and fill it with toxic gas."

"As proof of *your* insanity, we are going to set our house on fire and burn ourselves to death."

"If you do what you are planning to do, many innocent people will be killed."

"If you do what *you* are planning to do, many innocent people will be killed."

"Well, if that happens, I'll take full responsibility for what we do but blame you."

"I'll do the same."

"We seem to agree on an awful lot."

"Absolutely."

"Then let's get on with it."

"Amen."

"Amen."

"God works in strange and mysterious ways."

"You can say that again."

"God works in strange and mysterious ways."

On February 28, 1993, the Federal Bureau of Investigation and the Branch Davidians, two religious organizations, began a fifty-one day standoff at Ranch Apocalypse, the Davidians' compound in Waco, Texas. By *religious organizations* I mean organizations whose respective members "share a specific fundamental set of beliefs and practices."

How Come Every Time I Get Stabbed in the Back My Fingerprints Are on the Knife?

David Koresh led the Branch Davidians, who believed him to be the Messiah. His prophetic vision was based on the Seven Seals of the Book of Revelation and was a mixture of apocalyptic theology and secular survivalism.

Janet Reno led the federal agents, who believed Koresh to be mentally unbalanced. Her prophetic vision was based on the authority inherent in the official seal of the United States and was a mixture of apocalyptic theology and secular survivalism.

Despite pressure from the FBI to abandon the compound, Koresh and his followers refused to leave Ranch Apocalypse, where they had stockpiled an armory with over eight thousand pounds of ammunition and enough food and water to last several months. On February 28, more than one hundred federal agents of the Bureau of Alcohol, Tobacco and Firearms stormed the compound. Four agents and ten Branch Davidians died in the raid.

On April 19, 1993, a force of 170 FBI agents attempted to drive the Branch Davidians out of the compound by injecting tear gas into the building through large holes they had created with specially configured M-60 tanks. The Davidians responded by setting their compound on fire. Eighty-six Davidians perished in the fire, including Koresh and seventeen children. Throughout the episode, negotiations between the two parties were highly publicized. (This summary was adapted primarily from Lacayo, 1993, and Kantrowitz, 1993.)

The conversation that opened this chapter is a semifictional summary of statements I heard from representatives of the two religious sects during the developing conflagration in Waco, Texas. As I listened to the statements by the spokespersons of both groups, I became aware that the underlying patterns of thought, the basic value systems, and the organizational actions of the protagonists were equally bizarre and essentially identical. In short, they shared the same basic religion.

It's a conversation that I know is not altogether factual, but I believe that it is ultimately truthful. It made me realize that frequently those whom we call victims and those whom we term victimizers, whatever the organizational setting in which they function, both share and collude in maintaining dysfunctional ways of coping with their organizations' problems. The only factor that differentiates them is their relative power, with the role of the victim being awarded to the less powerful.

Also, I was particularly impressed by how staunchly each side, in its own unique way, contended that God supported its point of view. Ultimately, though, all the participants were victims, including God.

Finally, this experience has led me to understand that for organizational leaders and consultants to be effective, they need to know a lot more about the role that religion plays in organizational behavior. In the absence of such knowledge, their relevance is at best compromised and at worst destroyed by the systems they mean to serve.

CHAPTER ELEVEN

When We Buy a Pig: The Tragedy of the No-Nonsense Manager

Because you apparently are interested in the fields of management and organization, and because you apparently have hung on through discussions ranging from adventures with backstabbing to adventures in Waco (not to mention adventures in church), I know you *must* be interested in knowing about my health problems.

Ignoring for the moment whether the preceding segue has logical integrity, let me begin by saying that if it were not for the grace of God, a synergistic surgical team, and an Arkansas porker named Herman T. Dibbs, I wouldn't be here today. I'm not sure precisely where I would be. God willing, I wouldn't be in a climate that requires perpetual air conditioning.

To get to the core of the matter, I have an artificial heart valve. It is a porcine mitral valve, number AT 0899, model 6625, size 27. That information is both imprinted in my synapses and engraved on a laminated card I carry in my wallet. Given my ironclad memory, I am not altogether sure what purpose the laminated version is supposed to fulfill. Maybe if ol' Number AT 0899 suddenly blows a fuse and I fall on my face while waiting in line for a BLT at the local deli, a passing cardiac surgeon can find the card and shout, "Does anyone happen to have a spare porcine mitral valve, size 27, model 6625 handy? I need to drill it into this guy who's lying on the floor by the dill pickle jar."

In other words, I have been through open-heart surgery. Perhaps you have, too. I don't know what your experience was; I do know for sure that I learned a lot from my experience but that it wouldn't be first on my list of ways to achieve personal growth. In fact, Louis Grizzard spoke for me in *They Tore Out My Heart and Stomped That Sucker Flat* (1986) when he described it as something less satisfying than a Sunday afternoon picnic. I might even try sensitivity training first.

Nevertheless, despite its drawbacks as a developmental activity, I found that having one's heart carved on is not an altogether negative experience. Here is what it is like from my point of view.

They provide you with a limited wardrobe unsuited for those who tend toward bashfulness, load you on a gurney, and push you through a set of dented stainless steel doors into a surgical cathedral. Believe me, that room is not called a cathedral without reason.

Immediately you are surrounded by a group of masked blue-robed monks, who quietly chant rhythmic incantations taken from *Gray's Anatomy*. Simultaneously, they insert tubes in nearly every orifice of your body and create several new ones that didn't exist before they commenced their efforts.

Once they complete their chanting, they knock you out cold, take a buzz saw to your chest, and proceed to saw you open from your neck to your navel. They apply a meat cleaver to your heart, tear out the offending valve with large plumber's pliers, and replace it with a valve made from the irradiated tissue of a pig. They then close the gaping hole in your chest with staples similar to the massive ones Ms. Liebowitz uses to bind our university's lengthy annual report.

Once they are convinced they have your cover pages bound tightly enough to keep you feeling uncomfortable for a long period of time, they take you to an intensive care unit (ICU), where they keep you in a state of semiconsciousness for a couple of days. Then, after they have deprived you of sufficient sleep, they roll you out of the ICU to a private room so that you can begin your next stage of recovery.

Having been blissfully unconscious during the procedure, my description may lack medical precision when it comes to a few of the details regarding equipment and procedures. But that's what I am told happened to me.

So there I was—semiconscious, dangling tubes from every orifice of my body, stapled from my neck to my navel, the proud owner of a new pig's valve—being rolled to the promised land of a private room and a well-earned snooze. As we went through the door, I found my wife and, next to her, a hospital tray containing a full meal. My wife, I expected; the meal, I did not.

Although I was more than happy to see Beth, I really got interested in that tray. What in God's name did they think anyone in my pitiful condition would want to eat?

"Beth," I mumbled semicoherently, "take the cover off that plate of food, and let's see what's under it." She did.

It was a barbecued pork sandwich.

A welcome burst of adrenalin poured into my heretofore somnolent system, and I shifted from a state of borderline consciousness to one of acute mental alertness.

"Beth," I said, "do me a favor and ring for a nurse."

She rang, and in came a nurse. Not just *a* nurse, but an *experienced* nurse, a nurse who was old enough to be my mother. She wore a white uniform that was accented by a frilly lace collar and granny glasses. She had the look of someone who had been around awhile and knew more than a little about hospital life.

"Sir, may I help you?" she asked.

"Madame," I replied with more than a tinge of sarcasm, "Do you see any irony whatsoever in the fact that I have been unconscious for two days, have tubes dangling from every orifice of my body, am stapled from my neck to my navel, have a new pig's valve flapping around in my chest, and the first meal you serve me is a barbecued pork sandwich?"

She cocked her head to the right and looked at me . . . and looked at me . . . and looked at me. I could nearly see and hear the gears turning in her head.

Finally she said, "Sir, last week I attended a special program for nurses on the topic of cost containment. Now, when we buy a pig, *we use the whole damn thing.*"

242

How Come Every Time I Get Stabbed in the Back My Fingerprints Are on the Knife?

I started laughing so hard that she immediately sent for a resident physician to resedate me, probably out of fear that I would spill the monks' handiwork onto the floor and cancel out the gains in cost containment that the porcine reclamation project had provided.

It was with her comment that my bout with recovery *really* commenced. The nurse with the granny glasses captured both the seriousness and the absolute absurdity of the situation and expressed it in the good-natured, humorous way that Norman Cousins (1989) contends heals broken bodies and souls.

The Role of Humor in Organizations

Humor and laughter are indeed healers. But they are more than healers: they are important elements of managerial competence. In *The Managerial Grid,* for example, Robert Blake and Jane Mouton assert that the most effective managers use humor that "fits the situation and gives perspective" and, furthermore, that such managers "retain a sense of humor even under pressure" (1964, p. 4).

More than that, humor, or the lack thereof, is ultimately a spiritual issue. In *The Screwtape Letters,* C. S. Lewis describes hell as "something like the bureaucracy of a police state or the offices of a thoroughly nasty business concern" (1961, p. x). Consistent with that point of view, Screwtape, who in contemporary organizational parlance would be the director of training for aspiring devils, offers Wormwood, his trainee, the following advice about the role of laughter in organizations: "the phenomenon is of itself disgusting and a direct insult to the realism, dignity and austerity of Hell" (p. 50).

Finally, a recurring theme of virtually all literature on the topic of humor in organizational settings is that humor, laughter, and an appreciation of absurdity bring organization members together emotionally. Stated differently, they contribute to organizational health and member competency by preventing anaclitic depression, which as you know from Chapter Six is a form of illness-producing and sometimes life-threatening depression we frequently suffer when we are separated from or abandoned by individuals, organizations, or ideas we rely on for emotional support.

So my beloved nurse's pithy comment was not, for a variety of personal and organizational reasons, without positive consequence. She had fulfilled her organizational role as a healer and had done so with extraordinary competence. Would that all of us in managerial or support roles in our organizations be able to do the same.

The Tragedy of No-Nonsense Managers

My perceptive nurse's sage foray into the healing world of stand-up comedy again came to the forefront of my awareness a short time ago during an airplane flight, when I read

How Come Every Time I Get Stabbed in the Back My Fingerprints Are on the Knife?

a magazine article, the title of which eludes me, about a corporate CEO. What doesn't elude me, though, is a key element in the author's description of the CEO: he was described in glowing terms as "a no-nonsense manager." At first I thought the CEO probably was someone who didn't permit nonsensical organizational practices—those irrational, energy-sapping, soul-searing bizarre policies and procedures that are endemic to what I sometimes refer to as organizational phrog farms (Harvey, 1988c). As I continued to read, though, I realized that "no-nonsense" meant that the CEO had an unyieldingly serious demeanor and that he totally lacked a sense of humor.

According to the author, the CEO's lack of a sense of humor and his failure to appreciate life's absurdities were positive attributes, ones that all competent managers should express, emulate, and aspire to possess.

Since reading the article, I also have noticed in the "Employment Opportunities" sections of newspapers a surprisingly large number of advertisements seeking no-nonsense managers. Apparently, managers who lack a sense of humor are in short supply, so organizations are prepared to pay serious premiums in order to obtain them. As my colleague Erik Winslow so aptly described the dilemma, "The shortage of seriousness in management is no laughing matter."

In fact, given the apparent dearth of no-nonsense managers in the organizational community, I can foresee a day in the future when special management development programs are designed to teach aspiring managers the full range of skills and techniques required to abandon their senses of humor. I shared my absurd idea for this new breakthrough in management development with an acquaintance who turned out to be a no-nonsense manager. "Like hell you can," he replied; he then stomped away in a huff, thus giving credence to my worst fears and making Screwtape an even more worthy prophet.

I was beginning to feel downright depressed about the problem until I remembered a rather insightful but eccentric piece written by an obscure management educator, who said,

> Have you ever wondered why textbooks aren't funny? Have you ever wondered why the Bible isn't funny? . . . Likewise, have you ever known a competent professor, preacher, politician, manager, employee, or student who *wasn't* funny, who *didn't* have a sense of humor or an appreciation of the absurd? I haven't. For example, did Jesus ever tell jokes or pass gas in church? He must have. (He drove the money changers out of the temple, didn't He?) When He did, I'll bet that the disciples roared and God laughed. I just wonder why His biographers forgot to tell us about it. . . . By doing so, they destroyed part of His essence.

I suspect that is true for *no-nonsense* managers, too: an essential part of their humanity has been derailed or destroyed. Their spirits have been shrunk, and they are only tattered remnants of what once were whole people. In the language of political correctness, they are "emotionally challenged," and their competency to manage has been seriously compromised because much of our organizational life involves dealing with the kind of absurdity and nonsense for which the only sane response is laughter.

Try as I might, though, I can't get angry with no-nonsense managers. The line that separates "them" from "us" is much too thin, particularly during troubled times. I only can laugh and hope that they recover their precious capacity for fully engaging in nonsense before its palliative powers are lost to them and their organizations forever.

As you keep in mind the healing quality of nonsense, I hope you will also consider the possibility that engaging in nonsense is a requirement for coping competently with what Peter Vaill (1989) calls the chaotic world of organizational white water, a world that virtually all contemporary managers must face. That's why I think that much of the material in this book, frequently rife with nonsense, is much too serious to be taken seriously.

Consequently, let's mourn the tragic, limited, and limiting life of the no-nonsense manager. At the same time, let's celebrate the life of the manager who recognizes, acknowledges, and fully participates in nonsense, because that manager marches to the energizing beat of a very wise nurse who, thank God, has learned to use the whole damn thing.

AFTERWORD:
IN MEMORY OF SUZANNE

D addy, what if God is a mouse?"
My daughter, Suzanne, was seven years old when
she confronted me with that soul-rattling conundrum a little over twenty years ago. She did so during an otherwise
peaceful conversation between her and her thoroughly be-
fuddled father, who always had the uneasy feeling that he
was totally new to the job. Nevertheless, because of its enduring importance to me as a researcher engaged in exploring ethical, moral, and spiritual issues of organization,
Suzanne's query served as the focus of the introduction to
my previous book, *The Abilene Paradox* (Harvey, 1988c).

As I was working to complete this book, Suzanne died.
She went into her room one morning to take a nap and
died. Although she had long been plagued by several debilitating health problems, she died of a heart ailment that
was supposedly inconsequential. So much for the dictionary definition of inconsequential.

She was twenty-eight years old.

Throughout her twenty-eight years, Suzanne was never easy on herself or those around her, myself included. Regardless of the circumstances in which she found herself, she constantly asked unconventional questions, such as "What if God is a mouse?" As you might guess, questioning society's basic assumptions about the nature of the universe, assumptions that most of us take for granted while we read our newspapers and eat our corn flakes, is not an easy way to live. She constantly struggled with the big questions and was very content to let the small ones alone.

Suzanne was one of the least religious and most spiritual people I have ever known. She was not a church-goer. However, she did go into the backcountry of Ecuador, where she dug latrines for people who lacked both financial resources and, more important, hope. She did go to India, where she cared for dying children in one of Mother Teresa's hospices. She did go to the streets of Washington, D.C., where she distributed her homemade sandwiches to those who had no homes and who, without her, would have had no sandwiches. She did go to jail for protesting the violation of others' civil rights.

In Suzanne's view, God might be a mouse, but if so, God is a mouse who resides in the poorhouse, not the Ritz, and who nibbles on Velveeta, not Brie.

By the time this book is published, Suzanne will have been gone for a little more than a year. Although physically absent, she abides with me now, and she always will. I don't believe that a day has passed when I have not thought about her or cried for her. Yet, in the midst of the pain and sadness that frequently overwhelms me, I am so grateful for the blessings she brought to me. Indeed, God works in strange and mysterious ways.

As I said in the Acknowledgments, this book is dedicated to my wife, Beth. She is and always will be the love of my life. In consideration of what has happened during the past year, however, the book also is written in loving memory of Suzanne. God bless her. She now knows the answer to her question.

Amen.

Jerry B. Harvey

NOTES

Chapter Six

1. The anaclitic depression blues is a singular entity. Therefore, I follow it with singular verbs throughout the chapter despite the occasional jarring quality of the grammatical construction.

2. I am fully aware that my definition of anaclitic depression jibes only partially with the definitions one generally finds in the psychiatric literature from which the term originated. Most such literature describes it as a combination of turmoil and despondency that is found solely in infants who have been separated from their mothers or from mothering care. Given the limited (and limiting) scope of this definition, I am convinced that it was formulated by people who have *not* been abandoned at the altar, received a pink slip in the interoffice mail, experienced the misery of a corporate reorganization over which they had no control, or awakened one morning to discover that their communist economy had been replaced by a capitalist one. In other words, they have not experienced the traumas that can cause the anaclitic depression blues in adulthood. My definition of anaclitic depression encompasses people of all ages, not only infants. It also takes into account the fact that the blues can be precipitated by a broad range of experiences that involve being separated from important sources of emotional support. As we go through life, our mommies take many forms, only some of which have actual breasts.

3. Numerous studies have shown that being married is associated with lower levels of mortality; see, for example, Lynch, 1977;

Shurtleff, 1956; Trovato and Lauris, 1989; Hu and Goldman, 1990; Gove, 1973; and Lillard and Waite, 1995.

4. Although this finding is controversial, it has been the conclusion of many studies, including those cited by Lynch, 1977; Trovato and Lauris, 1989; Hu and Goldman, 1990; and Gove, 1973.

Chapter Seven

1. A bureaucracy, as defined by Elliott Jaques in *A General Theory of Bureaucracy,* is "a hierarchically stratified managerial employment system in which people are employed to work for a wage or salary; that is to say, a stratified employment hierarchy with at least one manager who in turn has a staff of employed subordinates" (1976, p. 49).

Chapter Eight

1. For a description of conflict resolution design interventions, see Walton (1987).

2. Jaques is fond of describing the relationship of the current professions of management and organizational development to groundbreaking management and organization theory (of which I believe SST is an example) as similar to the relationship of alchemy to chemistry (Jaques, 1989).

REFERENCES

Argyris, C. *Intervention Theory and Method*. Reading, Mass.: Addison-Wesley, 1970.

Argyris, C., and Schon, D. *Organizational Learning: A Theory of Action Perspective*. Reading, Mass.: Addison-Wesley, 1978.

Barnhart, R. *The Barnhart Concise Dictionary of Etymology*. New York: HarperCollins, 1995.

Barrett, W. *The Illusion of Technique*. New York: Anchor Books, 1979.

Bion, W. *Experiences in Groups*. New York: Basic Books, 1961.

Bion, W. *Learning from Experience*. New York: Basic Books, 1969.

Bion, W. *Attention and Interpretation*. London: Tavistock, 1970.

Blake, R., and Mouton, J. *The Managerial Grid*. Austin, Tex.: Scientific Methods, 1964.

Bowlby, J. *Attachment and Loss,* Vol. 1: *Attachment*. New York: Basic Books, 1969.

Bowlby, J. *The Making and Breaking of Affectional Bonds*. London: Tavistock, 1979.

Bradford, L., Gibb, J., and Benne, K. (eds.). *T-Group Theory and Laboratory Method: Innovation in Re-Education*. New York: Wiley, 1964.

Brandon, S. (ed.). *A Dictionary of Comparative Religion*. New York: Scribner, 1970.

Campbell, J. *The Masks of God*. New York: Viking Penguin, 1970.

Campbell, J. (ed.). *The Portable Jung*. New York: Penguin Books, 1971.

Campbell, J., and Moyers, B. *The Power of Myth*. New York: Anchor Books, 1988.

Campbell, R. *Psychiatric Dictionary*. (5th ed.) New York: Oxford University Press, 1981.

Carter, S. *The Culture of Disbelief*. New York: Basic Books, 1993.

Cousins, N. "The Laughter Connection." In *Head First: The Biology of Hope*. New York: NAL/Dutton, 1989.

Cronin, M., and Ludtke, M. "Wilding in the Night." *Time,* May 8, 1989, 20.

de Kruif, P. *Men Against Death*. Orlando: Harcourt Brace, 1932.

Elkin, S. *The Living End*. New York: NAL/Dutton, 1979.

Erikson, E. *Young Man Luther*. New York: Norton, 1972.

Gibb, J. "Climate for Trust Formation." In L. Bradford, J. Gibb, and K. Benne (eds.), *T-Group Theory and Laboratory Method: Innovation in Re-Education*. New York: Wiley, 1964.

Gove, W. R. "Sex, Marital Status, and Mortality." *American Journal of Sociology,* 1973, *79*(1), 45–67.

Grizzard, L. *They Tore Out My Heart and Stomped That Sucker Flat*. New York: Warner Books, 1986.

Guidubaldi, J., and Perry, J. "Divorce, Socioeconomic Status, and Children's Cognitive-Social Competence at School Entry." *American Journal of Orthopsychiatry,* 1984, *54*(3), 459–468.

Harvey, J. "OD as a Religious Movement." *Training and Development Journal,* Mar. 1974, *28*(3), pp. 24–27.

Harvey, J. "Abilene Revisited: An Epilogue." *Organizational Dynamics,* Summer 1988a, p. 37.

Harvey, J. "Phrog Index." Unpublished manuscript. Washington, D.C.: Department of Management Science, The George Washington University, 1988b.

Harvey, J. *The Abilene Paradox and Other Meditations on Management*. San Francisco: New Lexington Press, 1988c.

Harvey, J. "Broken Prayers and Organizational Un-Learning." In K. E. Watkins and V. J. Marsick (eds.), *Sculpting the Learning Organization: Lessons in the Art and Science of Systematic Change*. San Francisco: Jossey-Bass, 1993.

Harvey, J. "Class Syllabus for Management 210—Individual and Group Dynamics." Unpublished manuscript. Washington, D.C.: Department of Management Science, The George Washington University, 1997a.

Harvey, J. "Class Syllabus for Management 212—Behavioral Factors in the Process of Change." Unpublished manuscript. Washington, D.C.: Department of Management Science, The George Washington University, 1997b.

Harvey, J. "Class Syllabus for Management 290—Moral, Ethical and Spiritual Issues of Organization." Unpublished manuscript. Washington, D.C.: Department of Management Science, The George Washington University, 1997c.

Hu, Y., and Goldman, N. "Mortality Differentials by Marital Status: An International Comparison." *Demography,* 1990, *27*(2), 233–250.

Husserl, E. *Cartesian Meditations: An Introduction to Phenomenology.* The Hague: Martinus Nijhoff, 1970.

Jaques, E. *The Changing Culture of a Factory.* London: Tavistock, 1951.

Jaques, E. "Death and the Midlife Crisis." *International Journal of Psycho-Analysis,* 1965, Vol. 46, Part 2, 501–514.

Jaques, E. *A General Theory of Bureaucracy.* London: Gower, 1976.

Jaques, E. *Free Enterprise, Fair Employment.* New York: Crane Russak, 1982.

Jaques, E. *Requisite Organization.* Arlington, Va.: Cason Hall, 1989.

Jaques, E. "Basic Propositions About Leadership." Personal notes from "The Psychology of Political Leadership" seminar, The George Washington University, Washington, D.C., Jan. 12, 1990a.

Jaques, E. "How to Observe the Current Working Potential of Individuals." Unpublished manuscript, The George Washington University, 1990b.

Jaques, E. *Requisite Organization: A Total System for Effective Managerial Organization and Managerial Leadership for the 21st Century.* Arlington, Va.: Cason Hall, 1996.

Jaques, E., and Cason, K. *Human Capability.* Arlington, Va.: Cason Hall, 1994.

Jaques, E., and Clement, S. *Executive Leadership.* Arlington, Va.: Cason Hall, 1991.

Jenkins, D. *Semi-Tough.* New York: Signet Books, 1973.

Kantrowitz, B. "The Killing Ground." *Newsweek,* May 3, 1993, pp. 18–27.

Kennell, J., Voos, D., and Klaus, M. "Parent-Infant Bonding." In R. Helfer and C. Kempe (eds.), *Child Abuse and Neglect.* New York: Ballinger, 1976.

Kramer, J. *Lombardi: Winning Is the Only Thing.* New York: Pocket Books, 1970.

Kübler-Ross, E. *Living with Death and Dying.* New York: Simon & Schuster, 1997.

Lacayo, R. "Cult of Death." *Time,* Mar. 15, 1993, pp. 36–39.

Lewis, C. S. *The Screwtape Letters.* Old Tappan, N.J.: Macmillan, 1961.

Lifton, R. *The Nazi Doctors: Medical Killing and the Psychology of Genocide.* New York: Basic Books, 1986.

Lillard, L., and Waite, L. "'Til Death Do Us Part: Marital Disruption and Mortality." *American Journal of Sociology,* 1995, *100*(5), 1131–1156.

Litterer, J. *Organizations: Structure and Behavior.* New York: Wiley, 1969.

The Living Bible: Paraphrased. Wheaton, Ill.: Tyndale House, 1971.

Lynch, J. *The Broken Heart: The Medical Consequences of Loneliness.* New York: Basic Books, 1977.

Maccoby, H. *The Sacred Executioner.* New York: Thames and Hudson, 1982.

Machiavelli, N. *The Prince.* New York: Random House, 1950. (Originally published 1532.)

Magid, K., and McKelvey, C. *High Risk: Children Without a Conscience.* New York: Bantam Books, 1987.

Mallove, E. "Einstein's Intoxication with the God of the Cosmos." *Washington Post,* Dec. 22, 1985, pp. C1, C4.

Marrus, S. *Building the Strategic Plan.* New York: Wiley, 1984.

Maslow, A. *Motivation and Personality.* New York: HarperCollins, 1954.

McDaniel, E., with Johnson, J. *Scars and Stripes.* Philadelphia, Pa.: Holman, 1975.

McGregor, D. *The Human Side of Enterprise.* New York: McGraw-Hill, 1960.

Merva, M., and Fowles, R. "Effects of Diminished Economic Opportunities on Social Stress: Heart Attacks, Strokes, and Crime." Washington, D.C.: Economic Policy Institute, 1993.

A Midsummer Night's Dream. In G. Harrison (ed.), *Shakespeare: The Complete Works.* Orlando: Harcourt Brace, 1968.

Neilhardt, J. G. *Black Elk Speaks: Being the Life Story of a Holy Man of the Oglala Sioux.* Lincoln, Ne.: University of Nebraska Press, 1979. (Originally published 1932).

Nelson-Horchler, J. "Paying CEOs: How Much Is a Boss Worth?" *Current,* Dec. 1990, p. 12–14.

Noer, D. M. *Healing the Wounds: Overcoming the Trauma of Layoffs and Revitalizing Downsized Organizations.* San Francisco: Jossey-Bass, 1993.

Nohain, J., and Caradee, F. *Le Petomane: 1857–1945.* London: Souvenir Press, 1985.

Ornish, D. *Love and Survival.* New York: HarperCollins, 1998.

Peck, S. *People of the Lie.* New York: Simon & Schuster, 1983.

Peck, S. *A World Waiting to Be Born.* New York: Bantam Books, 1993.

Rabkin, E., and Silverman, E. "Passing Gas." *Human Nature,* 1979, *2*(1), 50–55.

Richardson, R. *Fair Pay and Work.* London: Heinemann Educational Books, 1971.

Rogers, C. "Personal Thoughts on Teaching and Learning." In *On Becoming a Person.* Boston: Houghton Mifflin, 1952.

Safire, W. "Calling Dr. Spin." *New York Times Magazine,* Aug. 31, 1986, pp. 8–9.

Scenitz, B. "More Than Ourselves: Havel's Declaration of Interdependence." *Newsweek,* July 18, 1994, p. 66.

Schacter, S. "Deviation, Rejection, and Communication." *Journal of Abnormal and Social Psychology,* 1951, *46.*

Schonfield, H. *The Passover Plot.* New York: Bantam Books, 1965.

Sham, L. "Mother Teresa's Heart Never Left the Poor." *USA Today,* Sept. 8, 1997, p. 17A.

Shurtleff, D. "Mortality Among the Married." *Journal of the American Geriatrics Society,* July 1956, *4,* 654–666.

Skinner, B. F. *The Behavior of Organisms.* Englewood Cliffs, N.J.: Appleton-Century-Crofts, 1938.

Spitz, R. "Hospitalism: An Inquiry into the Genesis of Psychiatric Conditions in Early Infancy: A Follow-Up." In *The Psychoanalytic Study of the Child.* Vol. 2. New Haven, Conn.: Yale University Press, 1946.

Symington, N., and Symington, J. *The Clinical Thinking of Wilfred Bion.* New York: Routledge, 1997.

Thayer, F. *An End to Hierarchy and Competition: Administration in the Post-Affluent World.* (2nd ed.) New York: Watts, 1981.

Trovato, F., and Lauris, G. "Marital Status and Mortality in Canada: 1951–1981." *Journal of Marriage and the Family,* Nov. 1989, *51,* 907–922.

Vaill, P. B. "Toward a Behavioral Description of High-Performing Systems." In M. McCall and M. Lombardo (eds.), *Leadership: Where Else Can We Go?* Durham, N.C.: Duke University Press, 1978.

Vaill, P. B. *Managing as a Performing Art: New Ideas for a World of Chaotic Change.* San Francisco: Jossey-Bass, 1989.

Vaill, P. B. *Learning as a Way of Being: Strategies for Survival in a World of Permanent White Water.* San Francisco: Jossey-Bass, 1996.

Vaillant, G. *Adaptation to Life.* New York: Little, Brown, 1974.

Wallace, C. *20,001 Names for Baby.* New York: Avon Books, 1992.

Walton, M. *The Deming Management Method.* New York: Putnam, 1986.

Walton, R. *Managing Conflict: Interpersonal Dialogue and Third-Party Roles.* (2nd ed.) Reading, Mass.: Addison-Wesley, 1987.

Watkins, K. E., and Marsick, V. J. (eds.). *Sculpting the Learning Organization: Lessons in the Art and Science of Systematic Change.* San Francisco: Jossey-Bass, 1993.

Wilson, A. *Jesus.* New York: Norton, 1992.

Wood, D., and others. "Impact of Family Relocation on Children's Growth, Development, School Function, and Behavior." *Journal of the American Medical Association,* 1993, *270*(11), 1334.

Young, R., and Veldman, D. *Introductory Statistics for the Behavioral Sciences.* Austin, Tex.: Holt, Rinehart and Winston, 1972.

Zill, N., Morrison, D., and Coiro, M. "Long-Term Effects of Parental Divorce on Parent-Child Relationships, Adjustment, and Achievement in Young Adulthood." *Journal of Family Psychology,* 1993, *7,* 91–103.

These pages constitute a continuation of the copyright page.

Acknowledgments

Introduction

Chapter One

Chapter Two

Scripture quotations are taken from *The Living Bible: Paraphrased* copyright © 1971 and are reprinted with permission from Tyndale House Publishers, Inc., Wheaton, Illinois. All rights reserved.

The excerpt from *The Illusion of Technique,* by W. Barrett, copyright © 1979 by Anchor Press, is reprinted with permission from the author's estate.

Chapter Six

The excerpts from *Executive Leadership,* by E. Jaques and S. Clement, copyright © 1991, are reprinted with permission from the authors and from Cason Hall & Co. Publishers.

The definitions from *Merriam-Webster's Collegiate Dictionary,* Tenth Edition, copyright © 1997, are reprinted with permission from Merriam-Webster, Incorporated.

The excerpt from *Child Abuse and Neglect* by R. Helfer and C. Kempe (eds.), copyright © 1976 by Ballinger Publishing, Cambridge, MA, is reprinted with permission from HarperCollins Publisher.

Excerpt from *The Making and Breaking of Affectional Bonds* by J. Bowlby copyright © 1979 by Tavistock Publications.

The excerpt from *Love and Survival* by D. Ornish, copyright © 1998 by HarperCollins, is reprinted with permission from the publisher.

The excerpt from *Healing the Wounds* by D. Nocr, copyright © 1993 by Jossey-Bass Inc., Publishers, is reprinted with permission from the publisher. All rights reserved.

The excerpt from *Men Against Death* by P. De Kruif, copyright 1932 by Harcourt Brace & Company and renewed 1960 by Paul De Kruif, is reprinted with permission from the publisher.

Chapter Seven

The excerpt from *A General Theory of Bureaucracy* by E. Jaques, published by Gower Publishing Company Ltd., copyright © 1976 and reprinted by Gregg Revivals, copyright © 1993, is reprinted with permission from the author and Ashgate Publishing Ltd.

Chapter Eight

The essay "Musing About the Elephant . . ." by J. B. Harvey originally appeared in *Festschrift for Elliott Jaques* by S. Chang (ed.), copyright © 1992 and is reprinted, in a revised form, with permission from Cason Hall & Co. Publishers, Arlington, VA.

The excerpt from *Free Enterprise, Fair Employment* by E. Jaques, copyright © 1982 by Crane Russak, New York, is reprinted with permission from the author.

Chapter Nine

The excerpt from *Intervention Theory and Method* by C. Argyris, copyright © 1970, is reprinted with permission from Addison Wesley Longman.

The excerpt from "Passing Gas" by E. Rabkin and E. Silverman in *Human Nature Magazine,* January 1979, copyright © 1979 by Human Nature, Inc., is reprinted with permission from the publisher.

The excerpt from "Mother Teresa's Heart Never Left the Poor" in *USA Today,* September 8, 1997, copyright © 1977 by *USA Today,* is reprinted with permission from the publisher.

The definition from the *Dictionary of Etymology* by R. Barnhart, copyright © 1995 by HarperCollins, is reprinted with permission from the publisher.

The quotation from *The Holy Bible* (King James version), copyright by Harper and Brothers Publishers (n.d.), New York, is reprinted with permission from HarperCollins.

Chapter Eleven

The essay "Ode to Waco" by J. B. Harvey originally appeared in *OD Practitioner 25*(4), Winter 1993 and is reprinted, in a revised form, with permission from the Organizational Development Network, 76 Orange Avenue, Suite 101, South Orange, New Jersey.

The definition from *The Random House Dictionary of the English Language (Unabridged),* copyright © 1983 by Random House, Inc., is reprinted with permission from the publisher.

Chapter Twelve

The essay "When We Buy a Pig . . ." by J. B. Harvey originally appeared in *Perido, 3*(3), May/June 1996 and is reprinted, in a revised form, with permission from the publisher.

The excerpt from *The Managerial Grid* by R. Blake and J. Mouton, copyright © 1964 by Scientific Methods, Inc., is reprinted with permission from the publisher.

The excerpts from *The Screwtape Letters* by C. S. Lewis, copyright © 1961 by The MacMillan Co., are reprinted with permission from HarperCollins Publishers Ltd.